FIERCE SOLIDARITY

Empowering Emerging Women to
Reject Physical, Emotional, and
Spiritual Abuse

ANNA E. TURNER

Little Hearth

Little Hearth
Sault Sainte Marie, Michigan 49783, U.S.A.

Little Hearth ISBN 9780692553176

Cover Photo © John Jevahirian

For Amelia and Juliette

May You Always Fly Strong and Free

FIERCE

Showing a Heartfelt and Powerful Intensity

SOLIDARITY

Unity or agreement of feeling or action, especially among individuals with a common interest; mutual support within a group.

Oxford Dictionaries

Contents

Acknowledgements

This book would never have made it out into the world without the help and presence of many good souls. Firstly, and perhaps most importantly, I would like to offer my deepest thanks to the people who mentored me through my adolescence.

Chris Baker is an exemplary minister, whose willing ear and gentle guidance helped me hold onto and develop my faith during challenging times. His example remains a guidepost for me on my journey toward agape-love. Chum Wollam was the first person to explain to me that God is not a man in the sky, among other liberating theologies. She offered sound, empowering, and often humorous spiritual guidance at crucial moments. Although she always used just the right words, it took many years before I understood the depth and full significance of all she taught me. Krisi Williams was my teacher, and a family friend. She has a knack for seeing the person within the whole while still valuing both. She knew my story inside and out, and kept me moving forward in spite of my aptitude for drama and wallowing. Finally, Robert Sloan, my teacher who went far beyond the call of duty. His availability when the going just got too rough literally saved my life. Without the life preserver these two dedicated teachers offered me daily through their brotherly and sisterly encouragement, their unwavering faith in my future success, and their longsuffering willingness to take me seriously, I'd be a statistic in a book on teen suicide. The interest these four people showed in my young life encouraged me long after the relationships were over. I will always be grateful.

Sarah and Curt, thank you for modeling a healthy, balanced relationship. Thank you for moving my things, for feeding me, housing me, and nourishing my spirit with joy and laughter and normalcy. Thank you for intervening for me. Thank you for not letting me fall through the cracks.

Tara Wager, thank you for guiding me down to face my darkest fears, and thank you for guiding me back up again. Anyone needing help uncovering and healing old wounds would be well served by her and the resources she's made available. You can find her at theorganicsister.com.

Barbara Eberle, thank you for holding a space for me in the world of ministry. Your work has given me a place to belong. My heart overflows with gratitude for you and the Peace of God Chapel.

My deepest gratitude to RJ, for drawing the fierceness to the surface.

Mighty women who shared your stories in this book, I am so grateful, and will always be humbled by the faith you've placed in me. Your bravery has inspired me to see this project through to the end. My hope joins your hope: that our stories have been given a purpose. Thank you for standing with me and saying so fiercely, "No more."

Oliver—partnership with you is the icing on my cake. I'm so glad we found each other. Thanks for the editing, the feedback, the pep talks, the strong shoulder, and your unending faith in me and this project.

Author's Note

The advice in this book comes straight from my heart. Using my experience and the stories of those who were willing to share as guides, I approached the writing as though I were speaking to a younger sister or my own daughters. What would I tell them? How could I prepare them for what I was not prepared for? What knowledge do I have that might help them avoid the long-term challenges created by abusive relationships?

Fierce Solidarity is not a book of research or professional insight. This is a practical book written from the perspective of a survivor to promote dialogue and awareness where they are most needed. I have written this book simply because I believe that what worked for me might work for you, especially if the knowledge is organized for you preventatively, rather than through recovery. My hope is that teens and emerging women will read this book and talk about it (or at least think about it). That they will speak up when someone is not treating them well, and pass on some knowledge to their friends. Ultimately, I hope readers will grow into the kind of women who are courageous enough to build lives of purpose and power.

The stories in these pages are real. They've been lightly edited for clarity, from personal interviews and autobiographical writings from the women who agreed to share their stories. For their privacy and protection, names and personal details have been altered. These stories are not included to induce fear. Rather, they are included to support your awareness and empowerment.

If you ever see one of these stories coming true in your own life, just remember, all of these women got themselves out of danger and are thriving now. Every single one of them are powerful, loving women today because they took the necessary steps to get out and rebuild their lives. This means that you can do it, too. Regardless of your current experiences, or those that lie behind you, you have what it takes to heal and move forward with power. I hope that all of you will see the symptoms of relationship abuse before it gets dangerous. If you don't, please know that if someone chooses to abuse you, it won't be your fault. Please know that you are never alone in your struggle. All of the women who shared their story in this book are there with you, and stand as fierce examples of feminine strength. Advocacy groups with loving, passionate people are out there solely to support your liberation and recovery from abusive situations. They want those in need to show up. It's why they exist. Don't be afraid or ashamed to use those resources.

I've been encouraged to broaden the scope of this work to include all relationship abuse, to be gender neutral, and to include research on abuse in LGBT relationships. I do not assume that all relationship violence is due to masculine aggression or that it is only found in heterosexual relationships. My desire is certainly to never exclude anyone. The overall hope of this work is that readers will close the final pages with a determination to treat themselves and others with kindness and compassion and to be better versions of themselves everyday while firmly rejecting mistreatment in any form from others. This is applicable to all people.

This book does, however, uniquely address the journey toward feminine empowerment. I do not wish to change that. I need to address what I understand the best. It is the most honest way for me to proceed with this work, particularly since it is based on experience rather than profession or study. That being said, my work with prevention and healing is not finished. I look forward to expanding my awareness of the broader impact of relationship abuse and how we heal from it. Any people who feel that their experience is excluded from the discussion in this book are welcome to contact me with their stories. You will find me at www.littlehearth.com.

Introduction

When I was in high school at the turn of the millennium, I could hardly fathom the idea of relationship violence sneaking its way into the lives of my peers. Most of my girlfriends were strong, intelligent, sassy, and headstrong. Whether we'd witnessed violence in our homes or not, most of us thought that abuse was really more the problem of older generations. Certainly the boys we'd grown up with, were much less likely to stoop to the lows of their fathers. We thought that gender inequality was a big deal, but not one that would affect our adult lives. After all, other women had paved the way for us. We could vote, we could work, and we could choose who we wanted to be. Abuse wasn't something that most of us were worried about.

Even so, according to the National Coalition Against Domestic Violence, the highest rate of relationship abuse within the United States occurs between the ages of 18 and 24 (ncadv.org), and looking back, I see this statistic reflected significantly in the lives of myself and my peers. Take a few seconds to think about all of your girlfriends and consider this statistic from the NCADV: one in three women have experienced relationship abuse in their lifetimes. One in three. According to these figures, odds are that some of your girlfriends or even you will face situations of abuse or violence. These acts of mistreatment do not need to be suffered in silence or seclusion. They do not *need* to be suffered at all.

I developed an eye for abuse and suffering as a child. It seemed that everywhere I turned there was evidence of it. When I grew into adulthood, having diligently worked to build a life free from abuse, I watched in disbelief as some of my childhood friends married men who mistreated them. Strong, smart, motivated girls. It was shocking to me that every single episode of abuse my husband and I reported during our long stretch of apartment life was denied. The abused consistently protected the abuser. More and more, I was seeing that relationship abuse had not gone anywhere. I was still surrounded by violence, and it was more complex than I'd ever allowed myself to understand.

Acquaintances told me stories of what had happened between themselves and their partners that made me sick with dread. "Do you think that's okay?" I would say. Most of the time the response was somewhat ambivalent and always noncommittal. Most often they said that they were going to stay with their partner, and offers for help or shelter were quietly rejected. Thankfully, some of them eventually removed themselves from their situations.

Most of my experience with domestic violence has been as a witness. The worst violence that my husband and I ever witnessed occurred when we were brand new parents living in an apartment. Late into the night, after our daughter was asleep and we were visiting with friends, we heard screaming. My husband, Oliver, our friends and I took off toward the door. Oliver lunged out into the hallway. I could see a young, crying woman crawling toward our door. The door slammed as gunshots were fired. So quick. So shattering.

It took about 15 seconds to snap out of the shock and remember that Oliver was in the hallway. When we cautiously opened the door, Oliver was kneeling on the floor next to the young woman lying with small bullet holes in her chest and abdomen. He and our neighbor, who had also responded to the screams for help had briefly taken cover in our neighbor's apartment during the gunfire. Oliver returned to the hallway when the firing stopped where he found the girl still alive, but fading fast with a look of utter shock on her face. He tried CPR, but her internal damage was severe and she passed away quickly.

We didn't know, yet, where the killer was. Oliver had recognized him as our neighbor, her boyfriend. He checked over the stairwells, then came into the apartment where we sat in vigil, waiting for the police to arrive. Our friend, ever present minded, had made the necessary calls to the police while I rocked and wept and prayed wordless prayers on the floor.

Once the police arrived they separated us, men from women. We were all questioned. Oliver was asked to identify the body in our neighbor's apartment. After firing many shots at his girlfriend with a semi-automatic weapon, he had retreated to his apartment and shot himself.

Making sense of what had happened was impossible that night. How could a young college sweetheart be lying dead on our doorstep? Even now I can hardly breathe for the thought of it. The response from the family of the young woman who died that night, which we followed through the local news and newspapers, felt just as disturbing to me as the act itself had been. It was difficult to discern in the days that followed. They spoke of their admiration for their daughter's boyfriend. They said he was a good kid. They even buried them next to each other. I was in disbelief. It was weeks before I could wash my hair without thinking about how she'd never wash her hair again.

We learned eventually through newspaper articles and her MySpace page (which became an online vigil for her friends) that the young woman who died that night had been uncomfortable with the relationship for some time. Friends commented on how she had been trying to distance herself for months from her boyfriend and was planning to break up with him for good that night.

This event was a heart wrenching reminder that relationship violence and abuse is so often invisible from the outside, and that those who do see what's happening often don't know what to do to help. Afterward, I was even more hyper-aware of domestic violence and its possible consequences than before. Somehow this event that occurred between strangers made everything seem so personal. It took several years, many more episodes of witnessed domestic violence, and a move to an area much like the one I grew up in for me to take some action.

Rather than spend my time thinking about how terrible domestic violence is, I realized that I *needed* to find a way to communicate, especially to those who have never experienced domestic violence at all, that it's really real, that it can be deadly, and above all: that it can be prevented. *Fierce Solidarity* is what grew out of that need. Increasing real awareness and teaching practical, peaceful resistance among youth population is a powerful way to create change.

The primary focus of this book is to help young women prevent relationship violence from becoming a part of their lives through self-empowerment. The secondary focus is to support young women in supporting each other by encouraging the development of active witnesses and sisterhood.

Most of us have the desire to help and fix. We do not, however, possess the ability or the right to change someone's life for them. The role of active witnesses is not to force or push change on others. A powerful active witness is one who is ready to emotionally support and practically help when a person in need reaches out. Another powerful way to help is to gently point out abusive behavior when we see it. As stories in this book demonstrate, simple acknowledgment of a person's situation can be a catalyst for change.

Active witnesses do not turn their heads away from suffering. They do not squirm in their seats when someone begins to tell their tales of trauma. They lean in and listen with big ears. That's how we sister each other. Pay attention. Listen. Help. This is an emotionally demanding way to live, which means that active witnesses must take good care of themselves. Active witnesses must learn to healthfully work through the impact of being a witness to trauma.

The same self-care and awareness that can steer you clear of abusive relationships can keep you strong and healthy as a committed active witness. With a community of active and prepared witnesses, more abused individuals may have the direction and support they need when they are ready for a change.

This is not a collection of stories of victims, but of women and girls who experienced abuse in environments and societies that allowed such abuse, then painstakingly removed themselves from it. It is imperative that abuse comes to be seen in an appropriate light. Not as something weak individuals bring on themselves or the actions of subhuman monsters, but as a product of damaging social conditioning.

Relationship violence isn't a saga acted out between victim and conqueror. It is something that happens between our neighbors, friends, and families. Strong people. Good people. People who are trying hard. It is very likely that people we know and love are either abusing others or being abused. We can work toward a more correct perception of abused people and abusers, but we must join in solidarity to support those who are healing from or resisting abuse starting right now.

Most importantly, we must be fiercely unwilling to either accept or commit acts of abuse ourselves. That is how we begin to turn the tide. Through a wide-sweeping, unrelenting commitment to healthy human relationships, we can stop this epidemic of woundedness in its tracks.

Each of us is born with the potential to develop deep and lasting relationships, to do meaningful work, and to experience life in all its richness. As you invest in a life intentionally free from abuse, you also get to invest in the life you want to be living instead of managing the fallout of an abusive relationship. Proactivity is much more efficient than recovery. If you have the opportunity to proactively protect your life from abuse, take it.

This book is intended to help young women steer clear of one of the common pitfalls of young adulthood by offering guidance toward growing into women who actively reject abuse in their lives. This small collection of stories about girls and women, all in their mid to late twenties at the time of writing, who experienced various forms of relationship violence at various ages includes an explanation of what to watch for so you can end a relationship quickly, and at the earliest warning signs possible. This assures that you can leave ample space, time, and energy in your life for growing into the woman you really want to be.

What is Abuse and What Isn't?
Developing a Realistic Vision of Love and Relationships

Deciphering the Grey Area

What is right and wrong rarely seems obvious in a black and white sort of way. Love and relationships are similarly complicated. They can't always be explained in definite terms. This is especially true because all relationships are different. People have different needs and express love in different ways. All of the flexibility that is required in a relationship can make it hard to distinguish a good relationship from a bad one.

This is never truer than when you're entering the dating world. The guy sitting at the front of the class who spends all his time playing games doesn't seem like much next to the confident, well-dressed type who stands out from the crowd only because of how gorgeous he is. But we all know that we can't judge people's characters by their appearances. It's worth noting that the guys many girls are attracted to: charming, arrogant or self-defacing, and seemingly ready for long-term commitment, can also fit the profile of prospective abusers regardless of their looks or social profile.

A little sweet talk and an "I love you" can go a long way for people of any age, especially those who are in the market for a partner. One important thing to remember, though, is that it's not unusual for a person with the potential to abuse to be in a rush for long term commitment in the form of promises, engagement, moving in together, or even marriage in a matter of just a few months. When you're looking for love and companionship it's so easy to get swept away in the romance of it all, but sometimes, once the commitment is secured, things turn ugly quickly.

In the introduction I described the murder-suicide witnessed by myself, Oliver, and our friends. It is a story of the extreme; what we tend to see as the very worst that could happen. But, most of the time, people live. Our hope is that individuals suffering from domestic violence live to tell the story of their abuse, pick up the pieces, reconstruct a sense of self, recover, heal, and become strong in themselves. Aside from never experiencing abuse at all, this is the very best possible outcome. Perhaps the worst outcome is that a person lives to relive and relive and relive abuse over and over again. It is a cycle that can seem impossible to remove yourself from, and if you finally do, another difficult journey—one of healing—has just begun.

Here is a true story from a young woman who experienced abuse from a very early age. This story demonstrates how quickly and easily you can fall into the clutches of the cycle of violence without even knowing it at first.

Carrie's Story

Carrie was raised in a home where her father dominated the rest of the family. There was no questioning him or his authority, and she learned early to be pleasing. As she grew into adolescence and adulthood, her life took some tragic turns into the world of emotional abuse and violence.

Anna: Let's start with the earliest episode of abuse you remember.
Carrie: There were episodes with my parents, emotionally, that I saw. My dad has always put my mom down, and has always controlled the things she does. All her life, my mom has had to ask

his permission for everything, and if he didn't like something that happened, or if she got back later in the evening than she had expected, he would say she'd been gone too long and then ground her.

"You don't need to go anywhere for two weeks. You're just going to stay home," he would say.

I'd only seen him physically abuse her a few times as a child. He smacked her once, and another time he grabbed her arm really hard.

Anna: Do you think your parents' relationship had anything to do with the pattern your relationships took?

Carrie: Yeah, I think whether I meant to or not I found a guy who wanted to control me, and then I found one again right after that was over.

Anna: What was your first experience of abuse like?

Carrie: As far as personally, what is most vivid to me begins with Jake when I was 15. Most of my relationship with him involved him being in control of things. He was in control of who I hung out with; when and where. He would tell me that no one else would ever love me as much as he did.

It didn't start right away. It was probably a month or two into the relationship, when all of a sudden it started. I think once I said I loved him, he kind of thought "*okay, she's mine*". At first it would start with him getting a little jealous about things. Then it became more frequent. He would ask where I was going and who I was going to be with.

We were together for a total of two years. It wasn't until after the first year when things started happening physically. The first time I remember him hurting me was during an argument. He had a really bad temper, and he was extremely angry with me. We were in a car parked somewhere by ourselves, as usual, because pretty much all he ever wanted to do was have sex. He grabbed my arms so hard during our argument that he left a massive bruise, and it just continued from there.

He would leave bruises, usually where you couldn't see them, usually on my arms and legs from grabbing them so hard. Recently I realized that there were many times when he sexually abused me. I would tell him no, and there was really no telling him no, because that's what he wanted. Eventually I would give in. He would either guilt me into it, or, I guess because I loved him, I thought I should just do it.

There were a couple of times when he really freaked me out. One time we had this huge argument when I was trying to break things off with him, and we were driving around some sharp curves. He started going recklessly fast. He unbuckled my seat belt and told me he was going to crash the car if I broke up with him. That really scared me, so I told him I wouldn't break up with him. I stayed with him a little bit longer and tried to break up with him again, but he would say awful things to me. *"No one else is ever going to love you."* Then he started threatening to kill himself.

I finally decided I needed to take care of myself and move on. I broke up with him on the basis of it being a two week break, because there was no way I could have completely broken up with him at that time. He basically harassed me during the whole break, even though I told him I didn't want any contact. He drove to my house and put a letter in my mailbox. After the two weeks I met him for a picnic and afterward I called him and said it was over. He threatened, again, to shoot himself, which never happened. Luckily, I moved soon after that.

Throughout our relationship he called me names and put me down personally, all the time. Bitch. Whore. He'd start throwing out names when he was angry, none of which had any basis at all. I became dependent on him somehow. He had given me a promise ring, and he had been my first sexual partner. Those things made it much harder to end the relationship.

Two weeks after I broke up with Jake, I met someone new who ended up being more manipulative than controlling. I had planned on giving myself time between Jake and Tyler. I had made a commitment to myself to just be single and go to school, to start something new, but that didn't happen. I think if I had given it more time, things could have been different.

I had gone up to visit a friend who worked in a bar a few times because I was newly free and could just go visit her any time I wanted. She told me one of the guys there was interested in me, and I said, "No, I don't really want to date right now."

She said, "No, he's a really cool guy," so finally I said I'd go, but only if she went with us. I didn't want it to be a date, date. So she, Tyler, and I went to the drive in movie theatre. I had a good time with them, so I continued to hang out with Tyler. He called me a lot, and we ended up actually dating. I didn't notice any trouble when we were dating. We didn't even argue.

Tyler got a job offer as a police officer in another part of the country. We had decided to let me finish my first year at the university and that afterward I would move down with him and get married. He wanted me to just move down right away, but I said no. I didn't think it was right to move so far away from my family, or to live with him before we got married. After a couple of weeks of him pushing me, I told him there was no way I'd move there unless he married me, and that's when he decided to ask me to marry him. So we did, like 3 months after I turned 18.

My wedding day, when I look back on it now . . . I cried all the way down the aisle. I don't think they were happy tears. He had already moved, made friends, and had a job by the time I came down. He was using the one car we had to get to work, so he told me he didn't want me to worry about getting a job. He wanted me to just stay home. He worked all day, every day. I would just sit in the apartment, cleaning and cooking. He wouldn't tell me when he would be home, and he'd go out drinking with his co-workers after work.

He wouldn't sleep with me, even as his newlywed. This went on for 6-8 months. At the very most we'd have sex once a week, and he got annoyed with me for asking him. I still don't know why, because before we got married he wanted it all the time. . . . you think something is horribly wrong with you. I had to beg him for it. Really for the first 8 months, he just wasn't around.

After that, he got a cop car from work to use as his own, so he didn't really have a reason for me to be home anymore. I told him I couldn't take it any longer, and I wanted to look for a job. That's when I started working. I think getting out helped a little bit. I don't remember at what point in the timeline it was, but I was having some problems with my appetite and energy levels. I went to my doctor who thought it might be my blood sugar. Eventually they diagnosed me with depression and started trying all these different medications.

Tyler and I started fighting all the time. We were never happy. I was finding out more and more things about him that I didn't know, like how much debt he had in his name, so we had to put everything in my name. He had money issues. He would tell me he paid bills when he didn't. We'd argue about it, but it would always come back to him yelling at me and putting me down. He would get right in my face when he yelled during arguments. He was a big guy, and I think I was already afraid of him then.

It finally got to the point where things were so bad, and I was in such a weird place . . . I am so ashamed of this . . . that I ended up cheating on him several times with a guy I worked with. I still feel terrible about it, because it's not like me. I just wanted something that made me happy. Tyler found out when he came home while the guy was there. It was terrible.

Tyler was extremely angry and told the other guy to leave. Then he kept shoving me up against the wall and yelling at me. I don't even remember what he was saying, but he was still on duty so he had to leave. That night when he came home, he threatened me. He said he could kill me and no one would ever know, because all of his friends were cops.

The next day he apologized and said he loved me. He said he was sorry for the way he'd been treating me for so long—which makes no sense to me now. I knew I didn't love him anymore, but the fact that I had screwed up so badly and he was apologizing to me left me feeling guilty and I just said okay.

Things were okay for maybe a week. He was nice to me that long. After that it just got really bad; the emotional abuse. Any chance he got he would put me down. At one point, I actually went into the bathroom and dumped an entire bottle of Tylenol down my mouth and locked the door behind me. He broke in and started digging it out.

So much of it I've just blocked out of my mind. He strangled me, threatened, yelled, belittled. When conversations got heated, I tried to just avoid him.

He gave me bruises from grabbing me like Jake had, but he never did anything to my face. Sex with him became very harsh. It was never enjoyable. Nothing with him was enjoyable—conversation, being in the same room, nothing was good. I don't know why he still wanted to be with me Even when I finally told him I was leaving, he didn't want me to leave.

Anna: How did he react?

Carrie: I left when he was gone. He had to go somewhere for work for a week. One of my co-workers said I could move in with her. I still don't understand a lot of it. Even after I hadn't seen him for nine months he tried to hook up with me when we met up one night in his car. I was trying to be real with him. I told him I didn't love him anymore.

Anna: What was your breaking point? What was it that made you decide you had to leave?

Carrie: I don't know. I think I discovered how much happier life was without him. I was working two jobs and hardly saw him. I enjoyed hanging out with everyone who wasn't him. After I moved out, I stayed with a friend for two or three months. I never saw him or heard from him. I went to pick up the rest of my stuff one day. I don't remember if he was there or not. I moved across the country then to start over.

Eventually Carrie moved back home, and went back to college. She was determined to earn her independence so she could start a new life. During this time she had a couple of relationships. Neither of the relationships lasted. For the first time she had been left by two men in a row. She had always done the leaving before.

Her stay at home had not been altogether pleasant either. Her father, who already had been controlling and domineering throughout her childhood, was undergoing a mental health crisis that made him paranoid and more violent than usual.

In Carrie's words:

My dad didn't like that I was challenging the irrational things he was saying, that I wouldn't just submit to him all the time. The tension had built up over time. One day he and my mom had been arguing a long time, and I couldn't take it anymore. They had made their way to the garage, and I was hearing noises, like tools hitting the ground. I thought he may be throwing things. I went to look out the window and I said something. He got in my face and threatened me about being in their business. He told me to stay out of it. I did. Later I had to go to work. I didn't want to cause any problems so I went out into the garage and said, "I don't have anything to say, I'm not here, I just need to go to work."

He got pissed off. He got over my face, literally nose to nose with me, spitting on my face as he was yelling. I said, "Dad, get out of my face. Get out of my face," and I tried to push him away from me. The more I kept moving back the more he shoved his face into mine. Then he grabbed ahold of my throat and started shoving me backwards and I kind of fell back sitting onto something. That's when my mom screamed and came over yelling, "No, stop! No, stop!"

He turned to yell at her then back at me. I think she had gotten him away from me so he was yelling in her face.

I got up and went over to them and yelled at my dad, "You need to stop or I'm going to call 911, this isn't cool, what's going on?"

My mom said, "You just need to go."

I said, "I'm calling 911." Then I tried to push my dad away from my mom. That's when he threw his elbow back at me and gave me a bloody nose. My mom tried to come after me to help and he shoved her down onto the cement floor. My mom was able to get up and help me into the house. She laid me down on the couch and took care of my bloody nose.

It took him a long time to acknowledge what he had done. He never really apologized, he just said, "If somebody's going to shove me, I'm going to shove them back."

After this, Carrie graduated from college, landed a good job, and moved out on her own.

■■■

Anna: What do you feel are the some of the long-term effects of being in these kinds of relationships? Do you feel you have worked through everything so that it doesn't happen again?

Carrie: I think I'm still working through it. A good portion of what I have worked through has just happened recently. Some of the long-term effects have been low self-confidence, not having my own opinion about things, or if I have them, not wanting to share them in a relationship. I've had a lot of discomfort with saying no sexually, too.

Anna: Do you feel that the way you were raised might have set you up for this?

Carrie: I would say that's part of it, only because that's all I saw growing up. My mom was always waiting on my dad hand and foot. She did everything he wanted her to, and believed everything he believed.

Anna: How did you feel about that as a little girl?

Carrie: I think I just thought it was normal. I don't think I thought anything about it until I saw my mom crying. Then I'd think *why is Mom crying?* I didn't understand it. The older I got I began to think it was kind of weird and that I never wanted to be in a relationship like that.

Anna: Were you free to have self-confidence and your own opinion as a child or was the pattern of men making the decisions already established as you entered into the intimate relationship world?

Carrie: It's definitely possible, I mean we weren't allowed to talk back or second guess anything. We were punished right away for that. We basically had to do what my mom did.

Anna: Did you feel like you deserved that type of treatment in any way?

Carrie: Yeah, I guess I always wondered what I did wrong.

~~~~~~

Carrie's may be a story that you think could never be yours, especially if you've not been exposed to domestic or relationship abuse and violence before. The reality of relationship violence does have the potential to affect us all, though, even if we do not come from a culture similar to Carrie's. Something to consider is Carrie's statement: "I thought it was normal." It wasn't until after she'd become an adult and had her own experiences away from home that she realized her parents relationship wasn't healthy.

There are unhealthy norms in every culture, so we all have blind spots. Carrie's cultural blind spots left her especially vulnerable to abuse. With a father who dominated the family and a mother who submitted to his mistreatment, the stage was well set for Carrie to expect this kind of treatment in her own romantic relationships. Expecting mistreatment might make it more likely to occur, but being able to recognize abusive behavior for what it is requires awareness and practice for everyone.

Even those who did not grow up in a culture that taught them to accept abuse have to work toward awareness. When we think of abuse, our minds often leap to outright violence. We might think that if there isn't any physical abuse that we're in a safe environment, but this isn't always the case. Carrie's story demonstrates perfectly how verbal abuse can escalate to physical violence. When we are able to recognize the precursors to physical violence, we are better able to protect ourselves from escalating abuse.

Knowing the Signs and Stages of Relationship Abuse

The First Symptoms

In Carrie's story, the first sign of the coming violence in her relationship with Jake was possessiveness and jealousy. Possessiveness is often overlooked as a sort of endearing quality. "He wants me to himself. He just loves me that much," are phrases that might run through someone's head to justify or even romanticize possessiveness. Girls might give up their friendships with other men or boys, thinking that they're being loyal, or even end friendships with females their partners don't approve of. Eventually, an abusive person can have their partner spending all of their time with him, dressing the way he wants them to, and giving up their personal interests to adopt his, all in the name of love. But this is not love. Love is not jealousy. Love is not possession. Love is not control.

Love cherishes, and values, but it is not ownership of another human being.

It's so important that we understand that possessiveness and jealousy are not positive attributes in a person or a relationship. They are a sign that the jealous partner has low self-esteem, even if that jealous partner is you. Only people who are unsure of themselves are interested in controlling other people, and it will never be possible for a relationship to heal this type of self-esteem issue. Individuals must work to heal their own self-esteem if they want to build healthy relationships with others.

Self-esteem is not about thinking you are better than everyone else. It's about knowing you are as worthy as everyone else. It's an understanding that you have value, as does everyone around you. Of course, we are all different, and our strengths and purposes are different. It's easy to get lost in the idea that some purposes are more important than others. This is made obvious in the way we tend to value this profession over that, or this skill over that one. The truth is we all rely on each other.

Coming to believe that your strengths and your roles are enough is a journey, one that can get tripped up so easily during adolescence and emerging adulthood. Not only are people who are coming of age trying to figure out who they are in the scheme of things, they are starting to trust in their partners and friends more than their parents. Many adolescents begin to question themselves in a way they never have before. This is natural, and odds are you're going to detour in directions you don't ultimately want to go. It's okay. Self-esteem is ultimately about staying committed to your sense of self, and seeing yourself as an equal. It is one of the necessary precursors to healthy relationships, because when you see yourself as less than others, it can lead to unhealthy, hurtful behavior.

Possessiveness, jealousy, and control are traits that are unhealthy for both you and your partner. Possessiveness is believing that you and your partner *belong to* each other. This is a problem because when something belongs to you, you get to do whatever you want with/to it. This is just not how healthy relationships work. Partnership can mean having *a place to belong*, but it never means you have ownership of each other. Think about the language of the seemingly innocent statement: "We belong to each other." Do people really get to *own* other people? No.

Jealousy, in a relationship, is possessiveness in action. "You can't hang out with him, because we're together." "That activity takes an hour of your time. I think you should quit so we have five hours together instead of four." This, of course, can quickly isolate you from the people you are closest to outside of your relationship, and isolation is dangerous. One of the major plays of a jealous partner is using guilt as a weapon. "If you love me, you'd want to be with me right now." "It hurts me when you go out without me." This can be extremely effective, because most healthy people want to please and nurture their loved partners—just not every second of every day.

Control is when a partner makes his/her own desires and discomforts into demands on the other partner. "I don't like that, so you can't do it." "Don't wear that shirt. It's too tight." "You can't hang out with those people anymore." "You need to quit that sport that you love." In one phrase, control sounds like, "You're going to do what I want you to do." How long do you think it takes for a person to begin losing their personal identity and power when they start giving into the controlling demands of their partner? Months, weeks, days? I think hours, or maybe even minutes.

You can make a safe sheltering space in your heart for your loved partner, but you can't hold them there through any means. The right person will want to be there often, but not all the time. Just because you love someone doesn't mean you have to be with them every free second of the day. Both partners need a life outside of the relationship. A possessive, jealous, controlling partner won't see this.

Checking for possessiveness, jealousy, and control in your relationships (in you and your partner) is something you can do on a daily basis. Even when these are the only negative factors in a relationship, take note. They are often overlooked, but the results can be devastating. People who experience this type of abuse can be separated from their friends, their families, and their dreams. When an individual is isolated in this way, it is much more difficult to seek help. Without help, it can feel nearly impossible to get out when the situation escalates. Right now is the best time to develop an eye for these types of behavior. Learn to steer clear of them, rejecting them forcefully when necessary. A person who has the potential to be a great partner will work toward trust, unconditional love, and flexibility in the relationship.

Here's a quick overview of early symptoms of abuse:

➢ **Possessiveness** is a sign of low self-esteem, and only your partner can improve his/her self- esteem. *Love is not being in the business of fixing people, so don't think it's your job to make someone feel better about themselves.* Possessive behavior is never a sign of affection. Love does not mean you belong to each other.

➢ **Jealousy** leads to isolation and control. If s/he's acting jealous, confront them right then and there and make clear that your value for them does not remove your value for others in your life. If the jealous behavior doesn't stop, end things, and don't look back. A relationship based on real love won't need you to give up your friends, family, faith choices, style, or interests.

➢ **Control** is when a person insists that their partner must do what they say. This leads to violence and is a form of truly harmful emotional abuse. If you find your actions or ideas are being manipulated or controlled, end that relationship as soon as you can.

An Affirmation: I am completely capable of developing my own ideas, opinions, and boundaries. My healthy relationships with family and friends are worth defending, as are my dreams, and my sense of self-worth. Even when I make mistakes, I am worthy of being treated with honor and respect. No one gets to define me but me, and I only choose positive words to define myself. I am whole. I am loveable. I am strong. I am worthy just as I am.

What it sounds like to reject control, jealousy, and possessiveness:

- ➤ "I'm going out with my friends tonight. I love being with you, but my friends are still important to me. If you can't live with that, then I think this is the wrong relationship for both of us."
- ➤ "My family has Sunday night dinners every week. It's important to me, and I won't give it up."
- ➤ "I love these jeans. I love the way they make me feel. You'll have to deal with the way other guys look at me when I wear them."
- ➤ "These guys are my friends. If you can't trust me, then I think we're in the wrong relationship."
- ➤ "I respect your religious choices, and I expect you to respect mine."
- ➤ "I don't like the way you speak about my friends. They were around long before you were."
- ➤ "You don't get to say when I can go out or who I go out with. If you can't respect my choices, this is over."

How would you stand up for yourself against possessiveness, jealousy, and control?

Moving On to Blatant Verbal Abuse

Another aspect of abuse is verbal assault. This could start by being slipped casually into conversation, perhaps a comment about your intelligence or strength. Or it could be worked into a disagreement. Regardless of what disagreements are about, they are threatening to an insecure, controlling person, and can escalate quickly into verbal and/or physical abuse. In Carrie's story there was a lot of name calling and belittling. We've all heard the expression, "Once you hear something so many times you begin to believe it." It is true.

Belittling can involve any theme that the abuser thinks will get to his/her partner and enable continued or future control. In Carrie's case, Jake chose words around the theme of whoring around, which played on her guilt about having sex with him in the first place. In Carrie's religious culture, premarital sex is a horrible sin. No doubt it was easy for Carrie to identify with the whore label, even though she was faithful to Jake and had been coerced into sex in the first place.

It is also worth noting that many cultures place more blame on young females than young males in situations of premarital sex since the males 'can't help themselves' when girls are dressed promiscuously or make themselves available. In many cultures, girls are used to feeling shame about their bodies, and are taught that they are responsible for not tempting men. Often this is part of a religious moral code. Girls are taught that virginity is not only a prize—it's *the* prize. It's clear that Tyler used this teaching to further control Carrie. In their world, she was spoiled goods. He easily sent the message that no good person would want her now that she wasn't pure.

Far too often, religious beliefs are skewed and manipulated by people who want control over others so that instead of being gentle guidelines that keep us safe and spiritually healthy they become bars that keep us trapped by other human beings. Sadly, it's effective. We all need to evaluate how our beliefs could be used against us by a verbally abusive person and refuse to allow another person to define how we should feel about ourselves spiritually, or in any other way. There is always a way back to peace and forgiveness. No person has the right to condemn you or belittle your spirit.

Verbal abuse is an attempt to claim a specific power over another human being: the power to define and manipulate another person's ideas about themselves. Verbal abusers then use that power to coerce others to do what they're told. Relentless name calling and put downs are often a part of abusive behavior, and as the abused begin to believe the things that are said about them, their sense of identity and self-worth crumble. This can leave them feeling powerless to remove themselves from the situation and even unworthy of independence. People who believe they have little worth are easy to control.

It is so important to guard ourselves against this type of abuse. We must internalize the truth that what people say about us is a reflection of themselves. It says nothing about us as individuals. If someone says something nasty to you or about you, they're not doing it to help you. They are doing it to feel powerful or surer of themselves. Every time you believe hateful things someone else says about you, you're giving away little bits of your personal power. It's important to shield yourself from that. Yes, we all need to grow, to be the best we can be, but having someone point out all of our flaws so we can feel really badly about ourselves doesn't help us get there. Only internal acknowledgment and a personal desire to be better versions of ourselves can motivate us to grow.

When we reject the negative things that others say about us, when we silence those who aim to control us and hurt us – to make us less in order to make themselves feel like more, we give ourselves the gift of honor and the space to see and hear within ourselves what it is *we* most want to improve upon. The purpose of seeing ourselves as strong and whole is so that we can grow into the best version of ourselves. The more we grow, the more we have to give. And so, rejecting verbal abuse is not only a gift to ourselves, but to those around us. The world needs us to be at our best more than abusers need us under their control.

Some Verbal Abuse Guidelines:

➤ Any type of **name calling is unacceptable**. Any person who belittles you clearly isn't with you because they value you. They are with you because they are getting something from you, be it sex, an ego boost, or a sense of control.

➤ Verbal abuse is emotional and spiritual abuse. It is an assault on the whole person, and it is not acceptable. **Verbal abuse consists of any words or phrases that attack who you are, your lovability, your capabilities, or your demeanor. It also involves the efforts made to make you feel guilt, shame, or responsibility for another person's actions.** If something is said that does not lift you up, clearly state that it is unacceptable and won't be tolerated. If it continues, don't tolerate it. Walk away no matter who the person is or how much you love them. You're strong enough, and you will find other people to love and support you without needing to manipulate and belittle you. And guess what. The world around you will be better for your strength.

An Affirmation: I alone am responsible for my own identity. No one gets to define me but me. I will not allow anyone to steal my joy, my sense of self-worth, or my personal power. My healthy boundaries are naturally established, and no abusive language may cross them. I acknowledge my faults to myself and work to take responsibility for becoming the best version of myself. I acknowledge my strengths with excitement and generously share them with the world around me.

What rejection of verbal abuse sounds like:

> ➤ "Woah! You don't get to speak to me that way."
> ➤ "Pointing out all of my flaws seems to be a fun game for you. It's not fun for me, and I'm not going to listen to it."
> ➤ "I don't do name calling. You can stop, or we can end this relationship."
> ➤ "I will not feel ashamed just because you think I should."
> ➤ "If I feel like I need to work on something, I will."
> ➤ "I respect your boundaries, and I expect you to respect mine.

Escalation to Physical Violence

As Carrie's experience with abuse progressed, physical abuse and violence became a normal occurrence. Once Jake had gotten away with controlling, manipulating, verbally assaulting, and emotionally abusing her, he stepped up to physical and sexual assault. It's clear that physical violence is always wrong, but some people find the lines of sexual abuse hazy.

In Carrie's experience with Jake, she was aware at the time that Jake was pushing her sexually. She felt she should always say yes because she loved him. It was also always wrong to say yes, since her personally held beliefs instructed her not to have premarital sex. Regardless, she did not have much of a choice, as he would not take no for an answer. What Carrie did not realize until later was that this was sexual abuse.

Sex can be so confusing, but mostly when you're looking for direction outside of yourself. The truth about sex is that it's wonderful, but only, and I mean only, under the right conditions: your conditions. What is most important about sex is that you have a clearly defined sense of what is right for you. Maybe those guidelines come from your religious beliefs, or maybe they don't. The important thing is to know your conditions and know what you're comfortable with, because under the wrong conditions, sex can be horrible; physically, emotionally, and spiritually.

Sex comes with a huge load of responsibility and consequences, too. It may be the first action we take in which our health and safety is entirely out of the hands of our parents. There are sexually transmitted diseases to worry about which may or may not seem like a huge deal, but the first time one of your friends tells you they've contracted something from their partner it gets real. You do not want an STD. Never, ever have unprotected sex – it's just not worth it.

A word on pregnancy risks that people don't often mention when they're trying to scare teens out of having sex: Your youth ends the moment you become a parent, and the loss of youth can feel devastating. Along with your youth goes a certain amount of freedom. Make that nearly all of your freedom. You'll have to make space for another human being in your life—and while babies are tiny, they take up a lot of space. They're like little vacuums. They suck up everything within their reach. Your energy, your money, and your time goes right down the baby shoot. Not to mention, everything is harder. It's harder to get to work, to school. Whatever your ambition is, you'll be carrying a baby on your back, and then bringing a kid along with you as you go. Your youth is valuable, and it's worth guarding and protecting. You're worth investing in for a good long while before you become a parent.

I think these responsibilities and potential consequences of sex are the very reason that sexual coercion is so very wrong. It is a very real form of physical abuse. Even if it doesn't leave you bruised or battered, if it feels wrong, then it's wrong. And there is no good reason to stay with someone who isn't honoring your sexual autonomy. If you are sexually coerced or assaulted, even one time, even if you aren't sure if it was actually abuse, please tell a safe person who can help you right away. If you don't know who that could be, you can always call a domestic violence hotline.

Some Good Rules of Thumb About Sex:

➢ If you're going to have sex, use a condom. **Every, every, every** single time.
➢ Only have sex when you can do so without guilt or regret afterward.
➢ Just because you said yes once doesn't mean you have to say yes the next time.
➢ Having sex doesn't make you a slut. Don't judge yourself or others.
➢ If you feel badly about having sex, you can stop and make new choices. Honoring your sense of right and wrong does not make you a prude.
➢ Healthy sex happens between two happily consenting individuals. When someone coerces another person to have sex with them when that person doesn't wholeheartedly consent, this is rape. Rape is not just physically forcing oneself on another. Rape is any circumstance where a person has been forced or coerced into sex. Rape can happen in relationships and in marriage, too.
➢ **You never have to say yes.**

Carrie's story depicts a relationship in which sexual abuse and manipulation was the norm. Not only was Jake having sex with someone who he knew felt uncomfortable with it, he was using guilt and shame to manipulate her further. This continued to play a role in Carrie's long term abuse. Tyler withheld sex and attention from her from the beginning of their marriage. Carrie thought something was wrong with her, which tells us that a lot of her sense of self-worth came from her sexuality. Then, at her most vulnerable, she made the decision to find encouragement elsewhere, an action that she could have felt affirmed all of those names Jake had called her in their relationship. Feeling so ashamed of herself at this point, she fell into depression and a cycle of vicious physical abuse, which now included harsh sex.

While Jake had power over Carrie's sexual life, he was also hurting her body elsewhere. We can see in both relationships that the abuse took a similar path. We can see the first abusive relationship's shadows in the next relationship as well. Then, when we consider the physically abusive experience she had with her father later, we come full circle to her beginning at home, where she learned the "correct" female behavior, which was subservience to the male sex.

Clearly, physical abuse is always crossing the line, but by the time the abuse had escalated that far, Carrie was so used to accepting mistreatment, that accepting physical abuse was a short leap to make. It is easy to say, "I would never let anyone do that to me," or, "that could never happen to me," but sometimes people find themselves in situations they could never have imagined. Sometimes abuse slips in so silently that it isn't noticed before something tragic happens. It can happen slowly over long periods of time or it can happen suddenly. In fact, it is very likely that most women who find themselves in abusive situations at one point also thought "that would never happen to me." That's why it's so important to diligently be on the watch for signs of unhealthy relationship patterns or changes, so you can get yourself out of the situation before it escalates.

Physical Abuse Overview:

> **Physical abuse is never, ever acceptable**. Whether it be a jerk, a slap, a punch, a pinch, a grip, a shove, a restraint, a hair pull, anything. Any intentional infliction of physical pain is grounds for the immediate end of a relationship, and no one gets to "take back" an act of violence or say they didn't mean to.

> **Your body is your own** to share only with whom you happily choose, according to your own personal conditions, beliefs, and boundaries. Any type of coercion or force is unacceptable and signifies a need to end the relationship.

An Affirmation: My body is sacred. I will protect it from harm. My body is mine to share with whom I choose according to my own personal conditions. I am clear about these conditions, and my boundaries will not be crossed without repercussions. My body deserves to be cherished and handled with kindness, and I will not accept any other type of treatment from myself or anyone else.

What defending yourself from physical abuse looks and sounds like:

> "You're hurting me. No. Stop."
> "I don't want to have sex right now. You need to stop right now."
> "This is not what I want. You're not honoring or respecting me."

Now, of course, ending physical or sexual abuse is not always that easy. These things need to be said not only to stop the situation from progressing, but because you will know that you set a boundary and it was crossed. These things need to be said as soon as you feel a situation might escalate. Then you need to get away as fast as you can. If you are in a situation in which you have to tell someone to stop hurting you, or in which someone abuses you physically or sexually, never, ever be alone with them again. Never get in a car with this person again. When you are in a car, you are isolated and portable. You have to stand your ground here, and protect yourself. Report it. Surround yourself with safe people who will defend you. Gather your Solidarity sisters. Meet in a public place to break up, or be somewhere that has many safe people around. Have friends nearby. Seek help from someone who can help you work through the traumatic event you've been through. Domestic violence advocacy hotlines are there for you, too.

Let's review the guidelines that you can depend on to let you know if your situation is abusive:

- ➤ **Possessiveness** is a sign of low self-esteem, and only your partner can improve his/her self- esteem. Love is not being in the business of fixing people, so don't think it's your job to make someone feel better about themselves. Possessive behavior is never a sign of affection. Love does not mean you belong to each other.
- ➤ **Jealousy** leads to isolation and control. If s/he's acting jealous, confront them right then and there and make clear that your value for them does not remove your value for others in your life. If the jealous behavior doesn't stop, end things, and don't look back. A relationship based on real love won't need you to give up your friends, family, faith (or non-faith), style, or interests.
- ➤ **Control** is when a person insists that their partner do what they say. This leads to violence and is a form of truly harmful emotional abuse. If you find your actions or ideas are being manipulated or controlled, end that relationship as soon as you can.

➢ Any type of **name calling** is unacceptable. **Any person who belittles you** clearly isn't with you because they value you. They are with you because they are getting something from you, be it sex, an ego boost, or a sense of control.

➢ **Verbal abuse** is emotional abuse. It is an assault on the whole person, and it is not acceptable. Verbal abuse consists of any words or phrases that attack who you are, your lovability, your capabilities, or your demeanor. It also involves the efforts made to make you feel guilt and/or shame, or responsibility for another person's actions. If something is said that does not lift you up, clearly state that it is unacceptable and won't be tolerated. If it continues, don't tolerate it...walk away no matter who the person is or how much you love them. You're strong enough, and you will find other people who love you without needing to manipulate and belittle you.

➢ **Physical abuse** is never, ever acceptable. Whether it be a jerk, a slap, a punch, a pinch, a grip, a shove, a restraint, a hair pull, anything. Any intentional infliction of physical pain is grounds for the immediate end of a relationship, and no one gets to "take back" an act of violence or say they didn't mean to.

➢ Your body is your own to share only with whom you happily choose, according to your own personal conditions, beliefs, and boundaries. Any type of **coercion or force** is unacceptable and signifies a need to end the relationship immediately.

Understanding these different forms of abuse is important as you work through the world of dating and intimate relationships. Knowing that there is a person out there who will love you for who you are, who will support you, and value you as you are is one of the most important things you can be doing when you're pining and planning for love.

It's also important to know that *all of it can wait.* You don't have to find the right person for you right away. I know that the desire for love and companionship is strong. It's a biological urge. However, you have plenty of time to settle down and do the relationship and family thing. The coming years offer you a chance to invest in yourself in a way that will be much more difficult to do once you are settled into life. Know that romantic love isn't urgent, and it will find you when the time is right.

What Healthy Love Looks Like

True romantic love isn't possible until we're really ready for it. It takes two whole people who already take good care of themselves and are ready to commit to living healthfully together. It means working at positive, healthy, open communication consistently, and with the awareness that it will always take work to make the relationship healthy.

It means developing a life that honors both individuals' needs and desires without judgment, fear, or limitation. It means trusting the other to keep their commitments and work to be their best self while you focus on keeping your commitments and working to be your best self. It means you know your weaknesses and work on them rather than pointing out the weaknesses of the other.

In a healthy relationship, there is no room for manipulation and abuse. Both partners have done too much work on themselves to ever accept abuse, and both partners are committed to doing no harm to their partner. In a healthy relationship, both partners understand that joy comes from the inside, and that it is not their partner's job to keep them happy. Above all, each partner is free to explore, change, and grow.

The guidelines for a healthy relationship aren't a set of rules about what the interaction looks like, or how much time you spend together, or who's responsible for what or whom. The guidelines are about being a healthy individual who chooses to be with another healthy individual. Between two healthy individuals, a healthy relationship can look a million different ways, but it will always be based on love and honor and a commitment to active kindness.

Honor in a relationship means:

I acknowledge with my words, thoughts and actions that you are your own sacred person.

Committed Love means:

We're in this together. We're always on the same side.

That is the goal of partnership. That may sound a bit dry, but it's just a foundation. Foundations are meant to be dry and solid. With the right foundation, the house can be as full of as much passion and color as you want. With the wrong foundation, the house will never do well no matter how much you try to patch the cracks, scrub away the mold, or level the floors. A healthy relationship is a shelter. It's a place to come in out of the cold, to be nurtured, valued, and protected from the elements. So a solid foundation is exactly what is needed.

The type of relationship you end up in will rely mostly on what you think of and how you treat yourself. So be kind to yourself. Honor who you are. Do what you love. Celebrate your wonderful self. Then allow the goodness that's generated to freely overflow into loving those around you.

Avoiding abuse isn't about being afraid of it. It's not about running from it. It's simply about being aware that relationship and domestic abuse is a real possibility. It's about rising yourself up within the realities of the world you live in. It's about empowering yourself to reject abuse fiercely if it raises its ugly head so that you can get on with building your good life.

Please take a few minutes to answer the following questions:

1. Have you or any of your friends experienced any of these types of abuse?
2. Do you feel that any of the behaviors listed in the above set of "rules" are acceptable? Do you feel that there is room for exceptions in certain circumstances?
3. Why do you think Carrie accepted the abuse in the first place?
4. Do you think you would recognize jealous behavior in a relationship as unhealthy?
5. How might your personal beliefs or faith be used against you?
6. At what point would you walk away? Where is your solid boundary?
7. What are your thoughts on the description of true love?
8. What are your thoughts on the description of a healthy relationship?
9. Are you in a rush to get there?

{2}
When You've Never Seen It Before
Becoming Your Own Advocate

Even girls that are raised in healthy homes are at risk of falling into abusive relationships. So many of us think that girls who have kind fathers and strong mothers with healthy relationships are home free. We may also think that girls with such parents understand the layout of a healthy relationship since they are the product of one, but this is not always the case.

Life can lead even the strongest people into vulnerable places. This is especially true when we're finding our way into the adult world. Nearly all of us have found ourselves in situations we never would have imagined, facing choices we never thought we would have to face.

The next story is about a girl who grew up in a healthy, supportive family. She grew up strong, independent, and driven to reach her goals. This is the story of how she fell into an abusive marriage and then worked her way out of it.

Becca's Story

"It was never really good from the start. Everybody saw it but me. You know how that goes. I was never really happy, but when Angie was born, things got really bad. As I began to branch out; started back to school, started doing more outside the home with Angie, it progressively got worse. The suppression. The mental abuse. He never hit me. It was never physical abuse, but it was the name calling, the putting me down, and that kind of stuff that, you know, you hear it enough and you start to believe it." -Becca

Becca: I was at the university for two, two and a half years, and that's when Mom and Dad moved. I went to visit for spring break, and I just felt like I was supposed to be there. I just loved it. At the same time my physician had diagnosed me with seasonal depression and put me on an anti-depressant. My best friend, who was my roommate and a sorority sister, and I had stopped getting along. We weren't even talking anymore. It was just terrible there. We'd come home and if one of us was in the living room, the other would go back to our bedroom and maybe come out after the other had gone to bed.

That was going on, and for some reason, when I visited my parents I decided I was going to move. I moved two weeks later. I had already signed a lease for the next year at the university, and I just. . . I don't know. It's all so weird to me. That's not like me at all. I started at a new university after I'd moved, and just a few months later I met Dan. I still call this whole period my dark ages. I honestly have no clue what I was thinking at that time of my life, because in high school I was dead set on being a career woman. I wasn't going to get married until I was in my thirties. I was set in my career, all of that, so how I changed, what changed in me...I still can't figure that part out.

Anna: It all happened very quickly after you moved, then?

Becca: Yes, very.

Anna: Did your ideals and your dreams change during that pivotal time?

Becca: No. I had changed my major because the new university didn't offer my preferred major, but I was still on the same career course. I wanted to travel— maybe go to law school after graduation—or get into politics, then eventually go back for a higher degree. My intentions were big at the time. Then I met Dan, and I don't know what changed. I remember telling him when we first met, half joking, that I was going to be the first woman President. I don't know if we were dating yet at the time or not, but he told me, "You don't want to get into politics, it's so corrupt. You're too good a person for that." That was the time period that I began to think about changing my direction. We started dating then, and our whirlwind happened. I ended up dropping out of school altogether to follow him. It was crazy.

It's all kind of a blur. In the beginning while we were dating, it was always okay. I don't remember anything really, dating wise. He was a lot older than me, so that played a part in things. It was after we got engaged, which was four months after we started dating, that the relationship really started to get worse. He started to change. He started to get controlling about things he did or didn't want me to do. I was supposed to study abroad for a summer. He didn't want me to do that, so I didn't go. Things like that. I would want to go check out a new place, but we'd always have to do what he wanted to do. The things I wanted to do were always an inconvenience to him.

I remember thinking I was happy and that I wanted to be with him. He gave me attention. He was interested in me and, since he was older, he wanted to settle down and start a family. I latched onto all of that kind of stuff, because I thought that was what I wanted and was ready for at the time. It still doesn't make sense to me, because I was so into having a career at the same time. I'm not sure where the idea that I was ready to settle down came from. I think a lot of the issue of falling into the trap with Dan was that I was just naïve, basically. I had no experience with abuse, and I just didn't think people would treat others that way. I was convinced—I mean—I was *set* on the idea that, no matter what, I'm going to end up in a happy marriage, because I grew up seeing how good my parents' marriage was. Being as young as I was, I didn't really understand that marriage, or any relationship, really, but especially marriage takes a lot of hard work. You don't just say your "I do's" and live happily ever after. It's not easy. It's work, and I think I was just so set on becoming a wife and a mother, thinking that was what I wanted. I was blind to what was really going on.

He started to say things like, "If I was to buy a ring what kind of ring would you want," and all those kinds of things. He went on a trip and he had called and I told him how much I was missing him. He told me when he came back we'd be together, and he inferred that he was going to propose, or talk to my dad about marrying me. Sure enough, when he came back he talked to my dad and had a ring. I guess that's where it all started. We didn't even know each other a year. I do remember feeling a bit of pressure to get married. I wanted a spring wedding. He wanted to get married sooner rather than later. I finally caved in and said, "Okay, fine." That right there should have been a warning sign.

Becca and I discussed the many reasons she may have wanted to be with Dan at the time. His age and the fact that he seemed stable and secure were big drawing factors. He also had an intriguing career that seemed like it would lead to a unique and almost glamorous lifestyle, which were things Becca had wanted to create as a part of her career path. She was in a difficult place in her life, though she didn't even realize it herself at the time. Life had taken a sudden shift and nothing felt sure; the career goals she was sure of only a few months earlier started shifting. It was easy to be talked out of pursuing her current set of goals in exchange for security and adventure. It also gave her the opportunity to be a part of something no one in her family had been a part of before. This new and exciting adventure of a life seemed to be unfolding before her, and she wanted in. Marrying Dan was a way to connect to something new that looked good. Though it is hard to come to terms with the fact that sometimes we make decisions that make sense at the time and then backfire in a big way, it really is easy to see why Becca made the decision to marry Dan at the time that she made it.

>>❖<<

Anna: Let's talk about what happened during your marriage, the bulk of the relationship. Was there a moment when you first realized there was a serious problem?

Becca: I remember before Angie was born thinking, "I'm not sure this is how marriage is supposed to be." There was one moment when I started to think, "Okay, this is just ridiculous." At the time we just had one vehicle. After we were married I didn't work. In fact, I didn't work for most of our marriage, so I was basically trapped at home. He'd drive to work, then he'd come home and we had our little routine. Well, there was a park you could go to close by, and I really wanted to go just to get out of the house. He promised me that on his next day off we'd go spend the day at this park. The day came and he basically told me, "No, I'm not spending my day off doing something you want to do. It's my day off. I'm the one that works. We're going to do what I want to do." Which was stay home, and for some reason that stuck out with me. It still does. I don't know if it was the broken promise, or if that was the first moment that I thought I knew it just wasn't right. Maybe it was the combination of the two. That was early on in our marriage, and I remember it like it was yesterday.

We would go out sometimes and make couple friends, but when we'd meet somebody I really got along with something would happen. He'd come up with a reason we couldn't hang out with them anymore. The first couple we really enjoyed hanging out with—the wife and I really got along. I just loved her. All of a sudden, Dan and the husband didn't get along, so we couldn't spend time with them anymore. Dan said the guy had made a comment he didn't like. It always happened like that, just something to keep me away from other people. It was terrible.

Anna: The seclusion factor is so powerful, and you were so young. At that age, we feel like we're women, but we don't know where the

49

lines are. We don't know where the line is between, "He cares about me, he wants me for himself, which feels good, and he's secluding me right now."

Becca: Exactly.

Anna: You've said that things got worse when Angie was born. What did that look like?

Becca: Yes, when Angie was born, I knew that I couldn't stay in a relationship like that, but I tried. I tried to convince myself that things would get better when Angie got older. I told myself that I needed to stay with it because Angie needs a family unit. I told myself all the things you tell yourself to try to make yourself happier, or to convince yourself that everything's okay. The truth was that it wasn't much of a family unit, anyway.

He never did anything with her, ever. He never would get up with her. I can count on one hand the times he changed a diaper or fed her or did anything like that—gave her a bath, anything. When she was a month old, he decided he was going on a trip for the weekend. I was so upset, because here I am with this brand new baby, she's not even a month old, and he's leaving me for the weekend. He told me, "Well, I work and I bring in the money, and it's your job to take care of the baby. It's your baby." That's basically how it stayed up until the day I left in terms of his involvement with her. I'd have to force him to do things with his daughter—take her to the park, go ride her bike, do something with her.

Anna: You said there was no physical abuse. Was there anything in particular that he harassed you about?

Becca: The big thing he would try to get me on was my parenting and my duties as a wife. He'd say, "You're not keeping the house clean enough. You're home all day, it's your job to make sure this house is spotless when I come home, and it's not," or, "Angie shouldn't be doing this, she should be doing that. This is your job. You're home with her. You're not doing your job as a mother." That's where he would really try to get me, especially with Angie. He knew that she was my world. She is my world, and so attacking my parenting was probably the best way to get to me. It probably still is.

Anna: So how did you respond to that?

Becca: There were a lot of tears. I would sometimes get angry with him, yell back at him. At the end of the day, though, I would end up apologizing for the way I reacted. There was never a mutual apology, though. His response would always be, "Well, now you understand. This is how things are supposed to be, so you reacting the way you do only makes things worse." It was never a two way street. It was always his way or the highway. He was always right and I was always wrong, basically.

Anna: So when you went back to school, what was his reaction to that?

Becca: When I first started talking about going back and finishing my degree he was supportive of it. Once it actually happened, he hated it. He despised everything about it. I was home, and he couldn't understand why I wasn't able to do my school work or take my classes during the day when I was home with Angie. It was all on-line, so I didn't even have to leave the house. He would complain that he would have to watch Angie for an hour or two so I could go to my seminars or work on homework or do whatever I needed to do for school. He absolutely hated that. As I got further along in my courses and became more and more excited about what I was doing and starting a career again, he would try to talk me out of it. He came home one day and said, "I met someone who does what you want to do today, and he said that you have to do this and you have to do that and it's just a terrible career path when you have a family because of all the hours and everything you have to do." He was just trying to change my mind. He would say things like, "Well, I'll hire you. Why don't you just work for our company?" I'd try to tell him that wasn't what I was going to school for, that it wasn't what I wanted to do. This was when I was finally getting pushed to my breaking point of standing up and saying, "I'm not putting up with it anymore. If I'm going to go back to school, I'm going to do what I've set out to do. I'm going to chase my dreams that I laid aside for the past 5 years, to raise our daughter, and do everything you wanted me to do. It's my turn now." He just wouldn't support that, and I think that's when I said enough was enough.

Anna: You said you just woke up one day and decided you weren't going to take it anymore. Had anyone approached you at all by that time about the way he was treating you?

Becca: Well, even before we were married, my parents saw it. I learned all of this after the fact. After the divorce. I wish they would have come to me then, and talked to me about it. Would I have listened at the time? I don't know. I was in such a state at the time I don't know what I would have done. It's so hard to go back and think you know how things would have changed if something had been done, or if someone would have stepped in. I do remember one time Dad was trying to talk to me. He told me he saw a lot of his dad in Dan, and he wanted better for me. That was it. I knew that they didn't really like Dan, for whatever reason, which now I know why.

There were two people who said things to me that really got me thinking. I was doing some babysitting out of the house for some people in the neighborhood at the time, and I got to be really good friends with the parents of the little girl. The father was more your typical guy, asking blatant questions about us early on before we got to be good friends. One day when he dropped his daughter off he said, "Well, I never see your husband. Where is he?"

So I told him, "Well, when you drop your daughter off, he's upstairs in bed. He leaves later, then comes home for lunch and he'll be outside or upstairs for about an hour, then he'll go back to work."

"Is he at all interested in the kids?" he asked. Through that kind of a process is how our friendship really got started, because that's when he discovered what was going on with me and how I didn't have a car, that I couldn't do things, and that Dan wasn't involved with Angie at all. Eventually he approached me and asked, "Do you think this is okay? Are you okay with this? Because it doesn't seem right."

I had always been thinking that it wasn't right. I had always kind of known, but I was waiting until I had a degree so I could go to work to support Angie and myself. I kept hoping things would get better, too. When this man questioned me, though, it confirmed all of those questions in the back of my mind. I knew then, that someone else was noticing this outside of my family. It wasn't just me, it wasn't just my parents being over-protective. Someone else from the outside world saw it, too.

Then, when I was coaching Angie's t-ball team, which Dan didn't like because I was out of the house, the president of the t-ball league helped me out. I was new to the league, whereas a lot of the other parents had older children who had played ball before. He talked to me one day. He said, "You know, I never see Angie's Dad at the games. Is he not going to help you out?"

Between those two, it was in the back of my mind that my feelings were not completely off base. It just gave me a little more solid footing in my thinking, and encouraged me to not put up with it anymore.

Anna: Yes, It gave you that crucial validation, because when you're in a place where you're being told that you're not good enough, that you're nothing, you shouldn't be leaving the house, that it is where you need to be, every independent thought that challenges those statements is questioned. Validation is crucial. So once you'd made your mind up, what was your next step?

Becca: I had to talk to my parents. It still gets me to this day how nervous and almost scared I was to talk to Mom and Dad about it. I knew that they would support me no matter what, and that they ultimately just wanted me and Angie to be happy. I knew they would support me in doing what was best for us, but I was so afraid that they would be disappointed in me. I'm a proud person, it's probably my biggest downfall, it was part of the reason I stayed so long. Some of my family members don't believe in divorce. I grew up in a Christian home, and my parents have been married so long. It seemed to me that I would be a failure if I had a divorce, and that it's not the Christian thing to do-to have a divorce- so I was kind of afraid of that.

I told Mom first, because Dad wasn't home, and she was very, very supportive. When Dad came home, though, and I told him, he said, "I'm so proud of you. It's about time." I was floored. At that moment I knew they had seen what was happening the whole time, and I'd just been putting up with it. It was a huge relief for me, because not only did I know my parents would help me get through it, they were proud of me too. I had been so afraid of disappointing them, but I think if they were disappointed in anything, they were disappointed in my choice in a husband and maybe my judgment there for a while. That was huge for me.

After Becca left Dan, she moved in with her parents for a while to get her feet on the ground. She finished her degree and landed an amazing job. Then she and Angie struck out to start a new life.

Anna: Do you feel like you're in a good place now?
Becca: Yes. Absolutely. I feel amazing right now. It felt so good the day I moved out. The day I finally got all my stuff—and I took so very little, I just didn't want it—and Angie and I drove out, that was the best feeling. Every day it's gotten more and more amazing. It started with that feeling of relief, of knowing I was out. Then the divorce process started which was another period of hell, with him trying to manipulate me and use Angie against me, all of that kind of stuff. Once that was finally over, finalized, that was another huge relief, because I was finally done with him, other than the custody thing. From that point on I've been so insanely blessed, and so insanely happy. I met a new man, and our relationship is the complete opposite of what I had before, and everything has just

fallen into place. I have this dream job that I thought I would never in a million years have. Even my dream of working downtown in an office building however many stories up has come true. It's been another whirlwind, but an amazing whirlwind! I can't believe all this is happening. Every day I think, "Wow, I can't believe this is happening, and it's good!"

>>Faith<<

In a series of courageous steps Becca took control of her life and set her intentions for what she'd always wanted. Until we make that declaration we can't move forward, even into what we most desire. We have to know that we've got something to offer, and we have to know we're worth whatever it takes to get to where we want to be. When we are being manipulated and controlled, our true potential is smothered under our efforts to live up to another human being's demands on us.

Many women in situations like Becca's have been taught that it is God's will that they should stay in a belittling situation and that divorce is an abomination in God's eyes. Fortunately, there are religious leaders who believe and teach that God does not want his daughters suffering at the hands of his sons.

In Becca's words:
During the divorce I struggled with the idea that I had broken a holy covenant to God. I believed God would punish me for taking this action, and I struggled with dropping Angie off at daycare since I had to work to support us when before I was able to be with her all the time. I just had a lot of feelings of guilt. I got involved in a group through church, and when we went to a women's conference, that was the first thing that we studied. They talked about how God doesn't punish us, we're just not following the path that he has laid

out for us, and sometimes it takes undoing our plans. The backtracking is hard until we get back to the path God has for us, and once we get back to where we need to be, the possibilities are endless. And that's exactly what I've experienced. That was my point of breakdown. I was sobbing because I knew this was exactly what I was supposed to be hearing and it related to me one-hundred percent. I finally felt like I wasn't a bad person or a bad Christian. I knew I wasn't being punished and ever since then, the blessings have been completely overwhelming. I needed that discovery that we, as women, are princesses of God, and we need to feel empowered by that. It was just very liberating. It was amazing.

Our discussion on hope for the future:

Becca: No matter what the situation is, there's always a way out. There's always a glimmer of hope, and awareness is critical. If you don't know the warning signs, what to look for, and what's not okay, of course you're going to fall into an unhealthy situation when it's presented to you because it's easy to get caught in the trap.

Anna: Right, and so often we belittle ourselves once we're in the trap. Why did I let myself get here? It's part of the cycle. It's how the situation evolves and how we can stay in it, because not only are we getting negative input from an outside voice, it becomes our own voice that we turn against ourselves.

Becca: Absolutely. You hear something enough and it's the only thing you hear. Of course you're going to believe it. Of course you're going to tell yourself it's true. I've used this before in trying to explain things—it's like that line from *Pretty Woman*, "The bad stuff is easier to believe." For whatever reason, that's so true, and it's especially true when all you hear is the bad stuff. You begin to believe it even though you know you're strong and you're smart and you know you don't have to put up with it. You start to tell yourself you are worthless and you don't deserve to be around other people. All of the crazy things they say, you start to say to yourself.

Becca's story is so important to share because in situations like hers she was in before she knew what she was in for. Having never witnessed abuse, Becca could hardly wrap her mind around the idea of someone treating another human being with such disrespect.

The idea that abuse is generational, that it happens mostly to people who grow up around abuse, may hold some truth. After all, Becca did not experience physical violence. However, believing that only people who grow up in homes with abuse are at risk feeds into this idea that there is a population that is exempt from domestic abuse and violence. That a girl who grows up in a good, strong, supportive, well-off family doesn't need to worry about marrying the wrong kind of guy. This is simply not true. Domestic violence is not prejudiced, so it is necessary that we *all* become our own fiercest advocates.

Let's take a look at why Becca ended up in a marriage with a controlling man. She had a strong family support system. She had goals and dreams. She was ambitious and independent. Not the typical image that comes to mind when you imagine the kind of person who will end up in a controlling relationship, right?

There are some prominent factors that stand out in Becca's experience that might explain why she fell into the snare of an abuser. The first is that a lot of changes were happening in her life. She was in college (which is one huge transition from childhood to adulthood in and of itself). Her parents had moved across the country. On top of that, her friendships were crumbling. Things in Becca's life were unstable. All of this emotional turmoil surfaced as depression.

Becca needed some stability in her life. She moved closer to her parents and began to weave together new ideas to reach her goals when along came Dan. Had he shown up a year earlier or a year later, Becca may have seen right through him. During this period of vulnerability, however, she was an easy target. This is not to say that we always have to be strong and have it together. Sometimes we just don't. What we can do during the times when we're feeling weaker, more vulnerable, or more confused is to acknowledge it and put off making important decisions until it has passed. It's also okay, during these times, to rely heavily on the perspective of those who know you the best and love you the most. Your siblings, your best friends, your mentors, and your parents really can see things from the outside that you may not. Just be sure you have a history of healthy support from the people you choose to rely on. It's never a bad thing to seek an outside opinion from trustworthy people.

This didn't happen in Becca's case, though. The manipulation started early and followed a similar pattern of abuse as Carrie's from the last chapter. Becca was already fairly isolated because of her recent move. What would get in the way of Dan's control over Becca were her dreams and ambitions. Right away he was able to get her to second guess her goals for herself, which was enough to get his foot in the door. He rushed her to marry him, all while she was still intent on having a career. Once they were married, he took complete control over her life.

Becca went from being an active young woman with huge goals to being trapped at home in less than a year. She had no say over where they went or what they did, and she was cut off from any friends she was making. It's clear how deliberate his isolation of her was. He wanted her to himself.

Next came the belittling. Becca, being an ambitious person who thrives on doing a good job, was vulnerable to his attacks on her "job performance." He belittled her ability to care for their home and their child, which was what she did at the time. Then when she finally got to the end of her rope and fought back, he used her loss of temper against her, putting her under his foot a little more. It took a great act of courage and determination for Becca to follow through with her plans to finish her degree. That one act of self-empowerment led to her eventual determination to leave.

Reflection questions:

1. Why do you think Becca fell into an abusive situation?
2. Do you think Becca's recent diagnosis of depression contributed to her decisions? Do you think mental health plays a role in the decisions individuals make about relationships?
3. How do you think you would have responded in her situation?
4. Do you tend to seriously consider the advice of your trusted mentors about your partners or do you prefer to be the sole judge of who is right for you?
5. How do you feel about vulnerability? Do you feel that you are a vulnerable person? Do you think that vulnerable people are weak?

Learning to be Your Own Advocate

Screening

One of the most important elements of self-advocacy is determining who to let into your life. So often this is based on attractiveness and commonality—shared likes and dislikes, shared values, faith, and political opinions. These things are important, but it's easy to have tunnel vision when meeting new people. An attractive guy might share your religion and your love of action movies, which sets him up well to be a great friend, but compatibility isn't enough to open the door to intimacy.

Potential intimate partners need to make it through another screening, which takes some time. The truth is that it's hard to tell whether someone is good or not. How do we know if someone really thinks we're "too good a person for politics" or if he's setting us up for a downhill slope into a world where he's the reigning sovereign or else?

Some people are so clearly not who we want to be with that we have no problem rolling our eyes and turning away when they "hey baby" us, but there are so many people in the middle ground. One small way to separate the good from the bad is to ask the simple question: *Is this person working with me or against me?*

For example: let's say that Becca met Dan and told him that she wanted to be the first woman president. Let's say that Dan actually believed that good people are ruined by politics. How would it have changed things if Dan had said, "I never see anything good happening in politics, but maybe I'm wrong. Maybe with the right person in there, things would change. Tell me about your ideas! How can I help?" That's an example of something someone who wants to work with you would say. A good partner will voice concerns and want to protect you. Ultimately, though, they will respect your choices.

A good partner comes with their own set of ideas, but they won't want those ideas to infringe on your actions. They're open to changing their mind. Especially in regards to your vision for yourself. If someone is setting themselves against you or your personal vision for yourself instead of helping create safeguards around potential concerns, it's a good sign to set them aside.

Is this person working with me or against me? Is this person willing to support my choices? Is this person encouraging? Is this person able to voice his opinions honestly without insisting that I agree with him? Is this person willing to encourage me even when he wishes I were making a different choice? Is this person supportive of me being the person I want to be? Am I willing to do all these things for this person, too? If the answer is no to any of these questions, move on. There is a person for whom you could

60

answer yes honestly out there. There is no need to settle. There is no reason to coerce yourself into a yes.

Boundaries

Screening a person to see if they would actually make a good partner is simple if you have well defined boundaries, so developing sound boundaries is an important element of self-advocacy.

Here are some examples of good boundaries:

- ➢ **Honor Your Standards.** If you have to talk yourself into being with someone at any point in the relationship, or if you have to convince yourself that a situation is okay, then the situation is most likely not okay. This is the "No Abusive Behaviors" boundary. If you can't tell for sure if the relationship is or could be abusive, you're better off ending it. Any other standards you have should be honored, as well. What is important to you? Honor your standards by ending relationships with people who do not match your priorities. You'll be doing both yourself and the other individual a favor.

- ➢ **Protect Your Dreams and Personal Vision.** If you have to choose between your dreams and him, choose your dreams. A real, loving partner will actively support your dreams no matter how ambitious or irrational others might think they are. Saying, "Yeah, you should do that, but now isn't a good time," isn't support. You want a partner who has your back and believes in you right here, right now. You want someone who will brainstorm with you and help you find the steps heading in the direction you want to go that are available right now. Don't forget the question: *Is this person working with me or against me?*

➤ **Protect Your Connection to Others.** Sure, everyone has a honeymoon period when all they want to do is stare into each other's eyes. Good times. However, if your partner is getting icy or manipulative when you want to hang out with your friends (male or female) and family it's a sign that your partner is possessive, and is likely to be jealous and controlling.

➤ **Guard Your Self-Worth.** Partners who make you question your lovability or self-worth are bad news. There may be periods of your life when you feel unlovable, when you feel second tier, and feel like you're going to be alone forever. Most people feel that way from time to time. What you do with those feelings, and how you take care of yourself during that time is what matters most. We are all loveable, and there are many, many people in the world that will find us attractive. It's your job to actively love yourself enough to walk away from anyone who tries to make you feel unworthy of love and attention.

➤ **Self-Advocate for Supportiveness.** Anyone who tells you you're not capable of achieving your dreams—big or small— is a mad person. You are more than capable. With the right support and enough ambition, you can achieve your goals. Develop the attitude: Either support me or get out of my way. The relationship that is worth fighting for is the relationship that supports you right where you're at. Yes, there will be hard times and times of sacrifice, but when you are about to give up your dreams or your purpose, a loving partner will pick up the loose threads and remind you of who you're trying to be. A loving partner won't ask you to sacrifice yourself. A loving partner knows that it won't serve the relationship in the long run anyway.

These boundaries all revolve around the abusive behavior we covered in chapter one. No possessiveness, no jealousy, no control, no belittling, no name calling, no sexual coercion, no hurting. Over and over again from every angle possible, no. Anything that does not look like love in action: No.

One Strike Boundary

There is a point, and you must choose it for yourself, at which you know you'll end a relationship immediately. No second chances. I think of this as the one strike boundary. Know that, at some point, someone will test your boundary. Some people will go as far as you allow them to. People have different limits for this boundary. One of my hopes in writing this book is that many, many people will set this boundary sky high. I do not want you to be abused, dear reader, but this is not about me. What does *your* boundary sound like? Let it sound like a sentence. One that comes alive, so that if that boundary is crossed your whole self will rise up against the person who dishonored it. If you love the person, that's what it will take to end the relationship. Your whole self will have to stand up and honor the boundary. *No one owns me. I am Mine. No one gets to belittle me. No one may harm me. No one pushes me around. Support me or get out of my way.* Whatever your sentence. Say it daily. Feel it. It's your boundary. It can help you save yourself.

That is what boundaries are about. They are about deciding what you deserve and diligently holding out for a partner, friends, and companions who will honor you. They're about knowing the warning signs to watch for, knowing when to pull the plug, and having the courage to do it.

Courage and Resilience

Ending an unhealthy relationship before it escalates into something worse, hard and heartbreaking as it is, is an act of self-empowerment. It is an act of being your own advocate, your own good-will ambassador.

Your friends and family may try to do this for you, but the warnings that come from family and friends are often over looked. It's easy to brush off their concerns, or to think, like Becca, "My parents are just being over protective." We must train ourselves to see the world and the people in it for what and who they are.

This is also true when friends, family, or other mentors push for relationships to remain intact even when they are clearly unhealthy. The important thing is to be willing to see situations for what they really are. Then we must be willing to always act for our own protection knowing that it is not selfish to take care of yourself. It is necessary.

Think of Becca's situation. Though many people in her family do not believe in divorce for religious reasons, no one would have been better off had she not acted as her own advocate. It is likely that her daughter would have shared her suppression with her, much like Carrie shared her mother's suppression in the previous chapter. Dan wouldn't have gained true confidence or security by having Becca under his thumb. It is more likely that his craving for control would have grown and his actions may have become more desperate. Becca's vitality could have slowly withered away.

When Becca began to see that what was happening in her relationship wasn't normal, that others noticed, and that Dan was controlling her, she took life's reigns in her own hands and changed her situation drastically. We are all capable of doing this; even, and especially, before we experience any type of abuse whatsoever. If we can learn to identify abusive and manipulative language, we can be our own advocates and walk away from unhealthy relationships before they escalate into abuse.

All of this takes an enormous amount of courage and resilience. It is not easy to stand up for yourself. It is not easy to choose to be single. It is not easy to defend your own honor, particularly when you've made choices you're not proud of. Fiercely practicing good boundaries can propel you toward courage, but you'll still have to take the active step of ending the relationship and advocating for your own safety and healing. I've walked this walk. I know what I'm asking of you. When it's all said and done, though, walking away early is much easier than letting an unhealthy relationship fester.

How to Break Up Safely

Breaking up is hard.   Especially when you are doing it to advocate for yourself against a person you still love. Even when you are so over someone, it's awkward to end a relationship. Let's break this down so that anyone who is struggling to break up can have a go-to frame of action.

1. Plan a time and place where you won't be alone.
2. Tell trusted people where you'll be and plan to meet them immediately after it's over. If the relationship has been violent or abusive in any way, have a friend with you or nearby—like in an adjacent room.
3. Show up, and get right down to it.
4. Say that it's over.
5. Briefly explain why.
6. Arrange a time to return belongings if necessary. Not alone.
7. Leave. A quick departure may seem heartless, but they're going to have to work through their feelings on their own. Sticking around will likely turn into an argument or a grovel-

fest, and neither is healthy. It's best to set immediate boundaries so both individuals can begin to reclaim their individual space.

Many abusive or potentially abusive people don't make it easy to leave the relationship. In fact, leaving an abusive relationship can come with enormous risk. If you are in an abusive relationship that you are fearful of ending, please seek assistance from a local domestic violence advocacy group. They can help you develop a plan to safely remove yourself from the relationship.

If you are ending an abusive, or borderline abusive relationship, but aren't necessarily afraid of your partner, please recognize that there is still a need for careful planning. Be ready to never be alone with your partner again. Be ready to have a safe exit plan when you end the relationship. Don't end the relationship when you are alone with your partner. Please consider planning to not be alone at all for a period of time after the relationship has ended.

It is so important to be careful about how you leave. Be resolute in your boundaries, and make every effort to protect yourself from an attack of any kind. Again, this means never seeing your partner alone again. It is better to overprotect yourself than to leave any room for him to attack you.

Reflection Questions:

1. What does being your own advocate mean to you?
2. Are there times that you remember when you knew what was best for you and you did it? How did things turn out?
3. What about a time that you didn't do what you knew was best for you? How did things turn out then?
4. What stops you most often from doing what's right for you?

5. Do you protect your dreams and visions, connection to others, and your self-worth? Do you honor your standards and self-advocate for supportiveness?
6. Are your personal boundaries clearly defined?
7. What is your one-strike boundary?

Choosing a Partner from a Place of Wholeness vs. Choosing a Partner from a Place of Brokenness

How many times have you heard it said, "You can't love someone else until you learn to love yourself?" It is said so much because it is true, but it can be a difficult concept to truly comprehend. Loving ourselves means always acting in our highest interest. It means knowing we're worth investing in, and taking care of. It's a way of life.

Actively giving love to yourself leads you to a recognition of your innate wholeness. For many reasons, though, we're often taught that loving ourselves is selfish, unrealistic, or even sinful. Some people are trained from a very early age that thinking of others first means giving until we are depleted.

When we act on these teachings, and combine that idea with what we are taught from movies and fairy tales and the like—that we'll find someone out there who will complete us someday—it's easy to fall into a pattern of believing we're broken and need someone else to fix us when really, we've just allowed our inner resources to be depleted.

The difficult part here for teens and young adults is that, so often during this coming of age phase of life, we *are* living on meager portions of the bare inner essentials like feeling loved, valued, and significant. It's so easy to feel unloved and unappreciated, as though no one understands us and we don't even understand ourselves.

The teen years are the perfect time to start practicing self-care precisely because life is and will continue to be full of challenges. Developing self-care skills during a time when feelings of insecurity and loneliness are typical isn't only helpful for the present, it also prepares you for the future. It's so helpful to have an array of life skills at the ready when those old feelings raise their heads from time to time, because they do for everyone.

Self-care doesn't have to be complicated or all consuming, it's just about making time to do things that make you feel stronger, healthier, and more like the self you want to be. Girl time, alone time, exercise, faith time, a good book, building something, a hot bath, a hike through the woods. Whatever sooths and empowers you. Take some time to figure what those things are for you.

Seeking the things that fill us up is about more than feeling good. Feeling good in the moment is easy. Choosing to spend our time doing things that fill us up and build a character that we are still proud of ten years later requires dedication. It's totally worth it, though, because the things that fill us up point us to who we really are. They shed light on our values. Actually doing those things is empowering precisely because we are actively engaging ourselves in becoming who we want to be.

Sometimes figuring out what fills up our tank is uncomfortable, because we don't think we're worthy of being like people we admire. *I'm not creative enough to draw. I'm never going to have the vitality to be a health and wellness person, so why should I go for a run today? I can't get a massage, because that's indulgent. I don't know anything about hiking through the woods. I'm so clueless that I'd probably get eaten by a bear. I'm not worthy. I'll never get to be that person.* When we choose to stop telling these disempowering stories to ourselves and start actually doing things that look and feel like the life we want, we show ourselves that we *can* be *that* person. In fact, we already are *that* person.

The more you practice this, the more you realize you are worth your own time. The things that are important to you become your self-care routine. The more you take care of yourself, the more you see yourself for what you are: *whole and able*. Then you get to reflect goodness through your identity and interests. And that is powerful, because when you're spilling over and reflecting goodness it nurtures everyone around you.

When a relationship begins with two people who already know they are whole and are taking good care of themselves, companionship is being chosen on a powerful level. Both individuals can be elevated and supported. Conversely, relationships that begin with two individuals trying to fill voids result in disappointment on all sides. Companionship has been chosen because being alone is painful, but romantic love isn't meant fill to holes. It's not meant to give us meaning or define us, and it isn't the source of our worth.

Healing Brokenness
Asking for Support – Honoring your Boundaries

There are many reasons why people sometimes feel broken. Maybe it's from abuse, maybe it's from goals that fizzled out, disappointment, heart break, parents divorcing, the death of a loved one, or major life changes. Romantic love cannot heal a suffering spirit. Soothing yourself when you feel broken with romantic love is like putting a band aid on a stab wound. You've covered it up for a while, but odds are, the wound isn't going to heal. When you've been deeply wounded, you don't need the medicine cabinet, you need the emergency room.

When you're feeling broken seek out the mentors who help you find your way back to wholeness. If you don't have any, try to find some. Even the best of romantic relationships won't fix your personal issues. You have to do that. Seek out the support that is right for you—a therapist, a minister, a wise friend, or a respected elder—and allow them to support you as you make the necessary changes in your life that honor your wholeness. Sit with the pain. Seek your answers with patience and openness. There is no other way. Healing takes time and effort and space. *We have to work for our own healing if we want it to result in long-term positive change.*

The best mentors hold space for you while you figure things out. What that means is that your mentors should not be people who push you into their solutions. They should help you protect your space. They should guide you to resources. They should supply you with inspiration. They should hold you up and keep you steady while you find your way back to solid ground.

Healing happens when we release control and take hold of responsibility. Control is attempting to force your life to be what you want it to be. Responsibility is meeting the weight and challenge of what your life actually is and responding to it. It involves surrender, creativity, and all the might you can muster.

I am responsible. I am capable. I can carry the weight of what has happened in my life. I can receive all the goodness that still exists in the midst of my pain, and I am worthy of it. I can creatively reflect that soothing goodness in my life for myself and others. How can I show up to life in a way that honors who I am? Living into that question openly and honestly will guide you to your whole self. It will show you what needs healing along the way.

It is vitally important that we release any attempts to fix others while we're working toward our own healing. It is far too easy to become a judgement centered abuser and perpetuate the cycle of brokenness, even if our intentions are good. What we think is good for someone else is generally a projection of what we really need to be doing for ourselves. Even if you clearly see that someone else has an issue, honor their humanity and realize that it's up to them to initiate their own healing. Even if it's affecting you. Everyone has to work out their own issues.

This does not mean you have to be a victim of other people's issues. You can protect yourself from the backlash of others who aren't taking responsibility for themselves. Boundaries work for this. It may be part of your healing to acknowledge someone else's issue and set a boundary to minimize its impact on your life. You can communicate the reason you're setting boundaries within your relationship, but it's never okay to give threats or ultimatums. Asking people to change for us is not only wrong; it's ineffective.

For example, saying, "I love spending time with you, but the way you act when you play violent video games is uncomfortable for me, so I'm going to do something else," sets a firm boundary and includes a plan of action that takes responsibility for your own well-being. It could also be the beginning of a helpful conversation. On the other hand, saying, "If you don't stop playing those stupid games, I'm leaving," defers responsibility to the other person, is a clear ultimatum, and is likely to start an argument. How we think about our actions and communicate our thoughts makes an enormous difference in how we feel about ourselves and how our lives unfold. You have the power to take action to improve your experience in your relationships. Taking responsibility for yourself and your experiences is an act of claiming that power. This is true with friends, family members, and intimate partners. *All* healthy relationships require good boundaries and personal responsibility.

It's remarkable, really, how difficult it can be to choose to think of ourselves as whole, and to take responsibility for ourselves rather than expecting others to meet our needs or validate our worthiness. On the surface, not asking others to change may seem like accepting unacceptable behaviors. It does not have to be that way, though; not when we set boundaries around the areas that just aren't working for us. Practicing this one habit is a radically loving act of self-care that is healthy for you and those around you.

When you've learned to love yourself well, then you are ready to love another. Make sure that when you are longing for love from another, that you are doing all you can to love yourself first. Take stock of how you're feeling overall. Think about how life is going in general. Are there specific areas you need more support in? Check in with your mentors, especially when life is giving you a whirlwind ride, like Becca was experiencing when she met Dan. During the times when it feels like our foundation is slipping it is essential to practice radical self-care. It's when we're at our most vulnerable that we need to be fiercest about advocating for ourselves. Often that means calling in our most trusted mentors to help us hold safe boundaries while we heal.

Reflection Questions:

1. What do you think about the phrase, "You can't love someone else until you learn to love yourself?"
2. Do you feel loveable? Whole?
3. Do you tend to think about relationships as being two halves making a whole or as two wholes supporting each other?
4. What are your thoughts on self-love?
5. Do you think it's possible to love someone else fully when you put meeting your own needs first? Do you think it's possible to love someone fully when you're not putting your own needs first? Why?
6. What fills you up? What are the things that soothe you?
7. Do you have a good idea of who you are and what your needs are?
8. What are your thoughts on saving people? Do you think you can help someone heal, even if they are resistant to or ambivalent about healing their wounds? Do you think it's possible to change someone?
9. To what extent do you take responsibility for yourself, your words, and your actions?

Putting It All Together
Awareness, Self-Advocacy, and Love

At this point, I'm hoping that everyone has a good idea about what abuse includes (not just physical violence, but verbal, social, and spiritual violence as well), what is abuse and what isn't, what the foundation of a healthy relationship includes, and how you can set yourself up for a healthy relationship by learning to treat yourself with loving care and by setting strong boundaries. We've covered recognizing warning signs, such as control and jealousy, as well as the importance of leaving early, before the abuse escalates. We've also discussed some guidelines to follow while dating or breaking up, and covered the importance of learning to really care for ourselves. Hopefully, you all believe that you deserve love in supportive and healthy relationships—starting with you.

When all that we've covered so far is put together, the formula for preventing domestic violence and abuse comes down to two key elements: **awareness** and **empowerment**. We need to be aware as individuals and as communities of the warning signs of abuse so that we can look out for ourselves and for others. Standing in solidarity is communal awareness. It means we have each other's back. We must all learn to earn trust from each other so we can stand together in good faith and confidence with eyes wide open.

We also need to be fierce advocates for our own self-empowerment and for the empowerment of others. We cannot help others who do not want to be helped, but we can support others who seek to take good care of themselves. We can help them defend their space and support their goals, visions, and passions; we can encourage them, catch them when they fall, and find people who will do the same for us.

We empower ourselves by meeting and handling the weight of our life. When people become their own fierce advocate, they

73

discover the real power within themselves. Empowered people see power as responsibility. They acknowledge the power they have in their lives and then commit to use that power responsibly, wielding it with the best interests of themselves and those around them in mind.

Disempowered people have been taught to be that way, and then they get stuck there either as an abused person or as an abuser. Disempowered people see power as might, or force. Abusers abuse because they are grasping for power to quell their fear and shame. This type of power distorts the person wielding it as much as the person who is being abused. You can't will empowerment into the disempowered. Both abusers and the abused have to seek empowerment within themselves, just like the rest of us. What we can do is always be ready to point people in the right direction. This doesn't mean we take their empowerment or healing onto ourselves. This means we teach what we know, while keeping our own boundaries firmly in place, and guide people to resources that will help them.

When we're in a good place, we need to be willing to give others a hand so that empowerment can spread. I believe the best way to spread empowerment is through example. If we embody empowered womanhood honestly, and that means being honest about our vulnerabilities as well as our strengths, we encourage others to start doing the same. Real relationships are forged. Sisterhoods grow. Within that safe space we raise each other up in powerful ways.

A word of caution here. We are not all counselors, and we shouldn't try to do a counselor's, social worker's, or intervention specialist's job. It's possible to do more harm than good without meaning to. Know when you've gotten in over your head and redirect the person who's come to you for help to the professionals in your area who are prepared to offer their trained assistance. Actually look the professionals up and carry information with you.

If we pair the professionals' capacity to safely intervene with personal willingness to help others with honesty and simplicity, I believe we can do a lot of good in the world. Kindness, compassion, showing up, noticing, listening; these things matter, especially to someone who is suffering through abuse. People need to be filled up with love so they can find the courage to take responsibility for their health and safety. As empowered people, we can offer love to people, simply by making an extra effort to embody kindness and encouragement. When we lovingly meet people exactly where they are, exactly as they are, without judgement, and start pumping them full of authentic, empowered truth and encouragement it works miracles.

This is much more effective than trying to push or bully others into doing what we think is right, which is abusive in and of itself. Bullying and pushing will backfire no matter how good our intentions are. Just remember that you can't save people. You can shower them with love, but you can't make them love themselves. So just do what you can and release the results.

We're going to be moving on in the next chapter to experiences of childhood abuse, which are especially difficult to cover. It is important to know if you're reading and you've already experienced abuse of any kind that it is not your fault, you are not alone, and help is available.

{3}
For Those Who Have Run the Gauntlet
Know you are not alone.

The following two stories may be difficult reads, especially if you can identify with them. Please keep in mind that these are real, autobiographical stories from real women who have worked hard to heal from their childhood trauma.

Megan's Story

"What doesn't kill you makes you stronger." My mom has been saying this for as long as I can remember. I am now at a peaceful point in my life where I understand what she meant. Looking back at the path that has become my life is extremely bittersweet. I can choose to think of all the amazing things that have happened to me and be proud of the person I have become...or I can focus on the painful experiences that shaped my life. At first they shaped me very negatively. Then I had a wake-up call and I learned I had no choice but to grasp those moments that make me cringe to look back on and put a positive spin on them. I was not going to become a prisoner of my past.

My first experience with domestic abuse/violence, that I can remember, happened when I was five years old...

My father was an extremely prominent businessman and to anyone looking in from the outside, we had the life most dreamed of. We had a beautiful home, amazing cars, the best clothes, always went on wonderful vacations and we had nannies and housekeepers. To most, this is the ideal life that they strive for. However, we all know that sometimes the package looks better than the contents.

My dad, he was someone loved by all because he knew the game. He knew how to put on a picture perfect show for others. Behind closed doors, things were quite the opposite. One specific day is burned into my memory, because it was my first experience with abuse.

My father had come home and the house wasn't in perfect condition. The housekeeper had the day off, and my mom had spent the day baking with me and my sister. There were dishes in the sink and the counters were dirty. To my father, this was a major problem. My dad started yelling the moment he walked in and was telling my mom that she didn't deserve nice things. She didn't deserve anything at all because she was a "lazy bitch".

He then grabbed her by the arm and shoved her against the counter and said she was going to watch him destroy things she loved since she destroyed his home that he paid for. He then instructed me and my sister to get a chair and stand next to the china cabinet. I remember that I was scared, I had seen my dad mad and yelling before, but never like this and never had I seen him touch my mom that way.

I was crying. He grabbed my arm and yelled in my face, "Dry it up, you are as pathetic as your mother!" He then had me stand on the chair next to my mom's china cabinet. Her cabinet meant more to her than anything. It was filled with beautiful family heirloom china. She would have me help her dust and clean it and tell me stories about it and how she would give it to my sister and me when we had our own homes. Sometimes when my dad wasn't home and

78

it was just me and mom, she would get it out and we would play tea with my dolls.

My dad screamed to me to hand my sister something, anything. I did and she took it to him and he smashed it on the floor, screaming and cursing at my mom. I remember hiding under the table and him yelling at my sister to get a piece and throw it. She didn't want to, but he made her. I just watched my mom bawling and begging him to please stop and not do it in front of us girls. He screamed for us to get to our rooms.

We ran and cried. My sister is older and she tried to comfort me and told me that dad gets mad sometimes and it would all be okay tomorrow. I heard my dad screaming and slamming things, and then I heard a door slam. Shortly after, my mom came in and cried and apologized, as if she had deserved it.

My dad was gone and mom slept in my room with my sister and me that night. The next day, my dad came home with a huge diamond ring for my mother and told us he was sorry and to pack our bags. He needed a break from work and we deserved something nice, we were going to Disney for 2 weeks.

My sister was right, everything went back to normal and everyone acted like the day before never happened. Other smaller instances happened and by this time, my sister and I had learned to just get out of the house or room when he seemed in a mood. The straw that finally broke the camel's back was when, one night, we heard screaming from my parents' bedroom. My mother was screaming for help, so my sister opened the door. My dad had a gun to my mom.

He looked possessed. This remains one of the scariest days of my life. My mom had blood on her face and looked disheveled. My father looked at us and told us to get the fuck out. My sister ran. I stood screaming for him to leave her alone...he looked at me and said "Do you think I am going to listen to you? You are as weak as your mother! You will be nothing just like her! What would you do without her?!"

It was at this moment that I was shoved out of the doorway by my uncle, my sister had went and called him. He coaxed my father to let my mom go. My uncle left with my father and we packed a bag very quickly.

We stayed with my aunt the next few nights and we soon moved into a tiny house with nothing but the one suitcase each of us had packed. I didn't see my father for weeks and my mom had talked to us and apologized for putting us through that. She said they were getting a divorce and we had no money so we would have to adjust to our new life. We would have no help and she would have to find a job.

I had overheard her telling my aunt that he told her if she is such a survivor that she could do it all by herself and she didn't deserve the shirt on her back. I thought it was so fun to 'camp out' and make tents in our room... now I realize we didn't even have a bed and my mom was trying to make it fun for us. She went to work in a factory and was on the way home one day when my father came up behind her at a stop sign.

He jumped out and was yelling and beating on the windows. My mom had put the car into park because at this point he was on the hood screaming into the windshield. She had forgotten that on her new car putting it into park caused the doors to unlock. He dragged her out by her hair and was bouncing her head off the hood of the car.

A trucker happened to be coming down the back road and helped her. He beat the hell out of my dad. He deserved it. He then held him down, had my mom call the cops, and said he'd take care of it and we better get out of there.

My mom talked with my grandma and we stayed there while she went to the police station to do paperwork. Mom came home, loaded us up and we left town. The cops had told her they could only hold him 24 hours and we needed to get somewhere safe. We went into hiding in a tiny town in a neighboring state.

We were there for 6 months and had gotten accustomed to life without dad. A few family members had visited but we never went back home. One day, we saw someone coming down the dirt road we lived on. They drove back and forth several times before stopping and talking to my mom.

She came back to the house terrified. We had been found by someone my dad hired. We packed up and moved again. After a few months in our new place, mom decided that we couldn't live life like this anymore. She told us she wanted more for us. We went back to our home state and I saw my dad for the first time in almost a year.

We moved back into the tiny house and my mom begged that he at least give us our beds, she didn't need anything, just for me and my sister. I remember waking up one morning after it had stormed through the night. I looked outside where our mattresses were laying in the front yard soaking wet. My mom was furious with him. Shortly after, the court ordered him visitation rights every other weekend but we all had to go to counseling and he had to do some anger management and parenting classes first.

Everything was fine, he brought his new 20-something girlfriend with him to pick us up for the first time. I hated her and noticed she was pregnant. All the visitations were okay and nothing eventful happened. Then he stopped showing up sometimes.

I learned by listening to my mom through the wall while she talked on the phone that he had become heavily involved in drugs and she didn't want us to go if he actually did show up. He had court documents so he was allowed when the time came. He eventually didn't seem to care anymore and I would go 6 moths to a year at times without seeing him.

His fancy job was gone, his appearance was gone, but his bitch girlfriend remained. She would tell me she was going to be my mom, that I was selfish like my mother, and that I needed to spend time with them because they had gotten married. My sister asked when and they said a few months ago.

I was 7 by this time and my sister was 12. He then landed another good job and was trying to talk us into moving in with him. He told us that instead of giving my mom a bunch of money he would buy us anything we wanted. He promised my sister her pick of any car when she was 15 to start practicing on, etc. Eventually, my sister went to live with my dad. The courts said she was old enough to make the decision.

At this point, my mother had been dating my now stepfather for quite a while. He wanted us to move and get married. I remember even though we moved to his town, he would drive me back to go to school, over an hour away, for the first year because he wanted me to adjust in my own time. I remember hating him, for no reason, other than he was a man. He was extremely nice to me and mom.

I remember watching my sister spiral out of control because my father let her do anything she wanted so she would stay with him. She was abusing drugs by 13 years old. My stepfather tried to talk to her and so did mom, but nothing would work. My dad had money and friends in the court, so nothing was done.

She was in a drug related accident when she was 16 in her little sports car. She was in a coma for weeks and the doctors had us say our goodbyes...but by miracle, she woke up. I think this was a wake-up call for my father. Things greatly improved from this point, but they were never okay in my mind. I watched him slip in and out of drugs and could tell if and when he was doing something, which isn't something great for a child to be able to do.

One day while I was pleading with him, he told me how worthless I was and how I was going to be nothing because I was so weak just like my mom. I learned to ignore it after that.

My personal experience of abuse towards me in a relationship and otherwise...

I had a wonderful and loving relationship with a boy named Will that lasted several years in high school. He was always a perfect gentleman and treated me so well. All of my family and friends loved him.

I was given the opportunity to go to France for the summer to be part of an exchange program. Will supported me 100% and thought it was a great experience for me. This experience changed my life and everything I had worked through with my father issues.

The trip wasn't as glamorous as most were told. I was raped by my "French cousin". He told me I was a little American whore, that nobody would believe me, that I was good for nothing else, and on and on while he did it. I reported it, but nothing was done. It happened again and I was moved to a different family because I didn't want to come home and the police wouldn't press charges.

I felt like a failure. I felt like I would be letting down my family and friends... like I really was as weak as my father always told me. I felt disgusting and like it was my fault for some reason. The nightmare ended and I came home. I didn't tell anyone.

For a few months I tried to act normal, but everyone could tell I was different. And I was. I was moody, depressed, and I felt worthless. I eventually told my mom, my best friend, and Will. He tried to be supportive and I just couldn't do it, so we broke up.

I spent many months in counseling again and got into a relationship with a guy named Brandon. Brandon was a charmer at first. After about a year, it turned.

He started with little things like telling me I needed to tell him where I was at all times, and I couldn't be around certain people. At first he did it in a joking way, but eventually he was dead serious. I stood up to him and he hated it, but it worked. I told him I would leave if it continued.

We were okay, but we did only do things with each other. Whether it was alone or in a group, we were always together if I wasn't in school. He was working 3rd shift and I would stay at his house. His room was in the basement.

I remember I hated that he would go out drinking after work with his friends (who did not have a good reputation) and I told him this. We got into a small fight and he was telling me all my friends were whores and that he didn't like me with them either. He said he was going to continue to go out with them and that I was being crazy. I left it alone and went to work.

He started 'accidently' locking the basement door when he'd leave for work. He justified it when I called him out on it by saying that I didn't need to be out whoring around. He heard I was going out after he left for work, that I was a piece of shit and was lucky to have him.

By this point, I had confirmed with several people that he was in drugs. Due to my father, this was something I was non-negotiable on. I told him I knew and this wasn't the life I wanted.

I was working during the day, and was taking college courses at night. I wanted a life where I didn't have to depend on a man and he hated that. He broke down crying and telling me he'd do anything, even go to drug counseling. He admitted he owed his dealer a lot of money and couldn't afford that or the counseling, so I paid.

I was so proud that he was getting his life straight, until I decided to surprise him by getting off of work early and going to the counseling place he was attending so we could go to dinner together. Mind you, I had been giving him money to go and he'd tell me about his sessions.

Little did I know, he only went the first time when we signed him up. He was taking my money and hanging out at his drug dealer's house! I couldn't believe it. I felt so stupid and betrayed.

I left. It was over. He began stalking my new house, calling me at work repeatedly, following me wherever I drove, so I had no choice but to file a report. They couldn't do anything besides talk to him until there was more of a threat.

I began dating Will again. Both of us had realized that we never got over each other. Brandon got wind of this and was furious. He called me one day at work and told me he was going to kill himself unless I met with him to talk, just talk, nothing else. I reluctantly met with him out on a country back road.

I got into the car and he grabbed me—he had never touched me like that before. He started yelling at me and it was like a flashback to my father. He smelled of booze. I told him to let me go and that there was no way that I would ever be with him again. He needed to get his life together.

Out of the corner of my eye, I saw a shotgun and an almost empty case of beer in the backseat. I knew then it was not going to end well. I tried to get out and he grabbed me by my hair, as the rest of my body was already out the door, he then slammed the car into drive and started dragging me along the road, holding me partially in by my hair.

I managed to punch him in the side of the face, which caused him to release his grip. He took off and I called his mother and told her he was out of control and not my problem; that I would get his ass put into jail if he so much as looked in my direction again. She was hysterical but thanked me.

I decided it was time to move. I needed a new start for my life. I had gotten great ACT/SAT scores and I had the ability to do whatever I wanted. Nothing was holding me. I had come to a breaking point in my life where I didn't want to be anywhere close to home...or the USA.

I began looking at colleges in England, because I had been there before and loved it. I needed a 100% fresh start. It happened to be August at this point and I was able to get into a great school that started the end of September.

It was a big shock to my family and friends, but I had been put past my limit. I made it clear, I wasn't running from my problems, but I needed to find myself and come to peace with my past. So, I picked up and started over.

My time in London was great until I had to come home to visit. My father told me I would never amount to anything. He said I was wasting my time and being selfish for deserting my family. It didn't matter how well I did or what school I went to, nobody would ever want me on their team. My sister echoed his statements. Surprise, they were back on drugs.

I decided at this point, I was going to prove everyone wrong. I was sick of all the negativity. I didn't deserve it. My sister ended up apologizing and telling me she felt lonely and like I didn't even want to be around her. I was honest and told her I didn't, she needed a new lifestyle for me to be part of her life. I wrote letters and pleaded with my dad to get help, he ignored all of it.

The London Bombings happened shortly after. The bus had blown up right outside my flat and I had seen the entire thing. I was traumatized. I finally was able to call home and spoke to my mom. I decided I should call my father because it was all over the news.

My father's response was "let's see how strong and independent you are now. You won't survive on your own. You will see that you need to be here and stop being a selfish spoiled bitch" I hung up. I wasn't a parent, but I could never imagine saying this to anyone, especially my own child when they have gone through something like that. Back to counseling I went.

I focused 110% of my time on my school work, proving myself to all the teachers, one who helped me get a job at *The Financial Times*, which was and is still huge. I was so proud to go home that Christmas and tell everyone that I was a Mergers and Acquisitions Analyst for one of the top companies in the world.

Everyone, except my father and stepmother, was happy for me and proud that I had made such a big accomplishment. The other two preached the same as before about how I would live a lonely life, and how I wasn't good enough to stay there. They told me the company was just using me and would eventually learn I am not smart enough for them. I couldn't believe it.

I continued studying and working as hard as I could, eventually getting into Harvard Business. I really thought, now this is the #1 school in the world... what can they possibly say negative about it? Well, this time I was back to being a selfish bitch because I was putting school and work in front of them and just because I was going there wouldn't mean anything in the real world. I couldn't believe my ears.

It hurts. Even when you are beginning to hate your own father you just want to be accepted. I saw at this point, though, that nothing I did would ever be good enough. I decided I had had enough. I told them until they went into rehab and got their lives straight I would no longer be a part of their lives. I would not call, write or visit. I would arrange to see my siblings and other family some other way. And I stuck to it.

Where things stand today...

I moved to another city, met Chris and got married. Chris works for the local government and at first I heard from my sister that this was a huge ordeal for my father because I was only marrying Chris to ruin him. It made zero sense and I ignored it. I couldn't understand how he was going to make even this about him!

Later that year, my father and his wife went into rehab. Part of their journey included making peace with those they had wronged. As much as I wanted to tell them to deal with it themselves, I wanted my father back. The one that was a loving person. Not the beast that had emerged.

Coincidentally, I received an e-mail from Brandon around the same time trying to come to terms with his demons. I decided to be the adult about both and encouraged their healing with forgiveness. Chris was supportive during the whole process, which helped.

For both, it will be a lifelong battle, but as long as two men and one woman have stopped their cycle, it is something big. It is a start. It will be a lifelong battle for me as well. I have trouble trusting, opening up, and showing emotion because I don't want to be perceived as weak (like I had been told I was for the better portion of my life).

I am happy to say that I am now happily married, have a son and another child on the way, and am a successful International Business

Manager. My family is and always will be #1, but my career is right behind. Not that I think Chris would ever turn into the man my father was, but I want to be able to be strong and capable of survival for just my children's sake.

I will never ever allow them to see a small sliver of what I had to. If I ever see even a small similarity of that nightmare coming out, I would be gone. No child (or adult) deserves to have to live through that. I am a survivor and always will be.

What doesn't kill you, makes you stronger.... if you chose to fight your battle and have the confidence to win.

Sarah's Story

I don't remember how old I was, for sure, but I was young - still in early/mid elementary school. The man who molested me, Frank, is my mother's relative. He and his family were close with my family - they came over quite often (nearly every weekend) to play cards with my parents, or we'd go to their house.

Often times my siblings and I would stay the night at their house. We would ask to sleep in the living room (there were 6 kids all together, as they had 3) but he would always say no, that the girls would sleep in their daughter's room & the boys would be in their sons' room. It never failed that, in the middle of the night, I would wake up to him touching my breasts (as if I had any then), my vaginal area or rubbing my thighs. I never let him know I was awake - always kept my eyes closed, never spoke to him...I would roll over but he always rolled me back over, whispering, "It's okay."

This happened every time we stayed at their house. My parents had no idea what was going on so they had him babysit us a time or two, while they ran a quick errand. When he would watch us he always wanted to play a couple of "games" with my sister and I. One "game" was, he would sit on the floor and my sister and I were to jump over him. As I would jump over him, he would raise his hand to rub against my vagina.

This went on for several years. I was in junior high school and I was sick of it and every time he touched me I would tell him, "Don't touch me!" Of course, he didn't listen because I allowed him to touch me for all of those years. At this point, he no longer touched me like he used to but, instead, he would rub my arm or leg, I was done with him. I had enough and slugged him. It hurt and I could tell - thankfully my brother taught me how to punch because that punch stopped his disgusting behavior.

I finally told my parents and my husband, Abe, about 5-6 years ago. Abe and I went to a seminar and I just felt the need to tell people. I wrote my parents a letter and let Abe read it before I sent it. My parents talked to a Sheriff to seek her advice. She gave them a name and number for a local detective who I had to talk to.

Since I'd put it in the back of my mind for so long, I was only able to give him the information I'm giving you...which was not enough for legal action. It was enough, however, for local authorities to keep him under close watch and for many locals to hear, through the grapevine, about what he was being accused of.

This all happened to my sister too - for a longer period of time, and he did more to her than me. There have been multiple girls, his own daughter included. I have since forgiven him for doing what he did, but there is absolutely no excuse for his behavior. His wife knows what went on and she continues to defend him.

Long term, it has affected my intimacy with Abe. Certain things he does, I will stop him because it just makes me feel sick to my stomach after a bit. He understands though and doesn't hold it against me. I'm also very cautious of my children. I know how I acted while all of this was happening and felt I had nobody to go to so I watch their behavior. I make sure I always tell them that nobody is allowed to spank them, talk to them badly, touch them in any inappropriate ways, etc.

I don't want my kids to be afraid to come to me. However, I know that that isn't always going to be the case. I was afraid to go to my parents because I thought if he knew that I was awake during what he was doing that he would do something even worse. My sister never told because she says he threatened to kill either her or my parents if she did.

With the kids, I ask them, daily what they did at the sitters. I ask them if she, or anyone else, touched them inappropriately. I'm always reminding him that absolutely nobody is allowed to hit or spank him or to touch him in his 'private' places. I reassure them that it is okay to tell me if anyone does these things, especially if someone tells them not to tell me.

I'm not sure what to tell others who have or are going through this. I mean, it's easy for me to say, now, that they should definitely talk to someone about it but before I told anyone, it was really difficult for me to be able to tell anyone. I had to get in touch with God in order to forgive myself and the one who molested me before I was comfortable enough to tell anyone. And even then (and now) I'm not comfortable to talk about it, in person. I have to write it down. The only way I was able to tell my parents and husband was in a written letter.

When I was a kid, I did think about it often. My parents were good friends with these people so we would see them every weekend. Even though Frank didn't touch me every time he was over, the way he spoke to me and looked at me still gives me the heebie geebies. He would talk to me and look at me in a way a guy does to his new girlfriend.

What I went through still bothers me to this day. If Abe and I are intimate, there are times I will push him away or stop him from doing something because flashbacks of Frank will pop into my head.

I don't know that I have a lot of advice for elementary aged girls but more for their parents. Talk to your kids. Ask questions. Be cautious of body language. I didn't really have a close relationship with my parents, so I didn't feel comfortable talking to them about this. My parents never had the sex talk with me so I was really uncomfortable talking to them about sex.

Child Abuse
And Healing From It

There is nothing harder to hear than stories of child abuse. It's horrific, and sadly, not as uncommon as it should be. Sarah's and Megan's stories are deeply mournful, but they also are a celebration of the resilience of human beings and the will to heal and begin again. Before I dig into the bulk of this chapter, I want to spend just a little time on child abuse for those of you who are in or have been in abusive situations in your home.

For children who have experienced and witnessed abuse, the world is an uncertain place. Just as they never know what to expect when they are around their abuser, they learn to not trust the world and the people in it to be consistent either. Rather, they expect it not to be. Children who know there is abuse in their home often feel like they are to blame, that they are flawed somehow, and they will try hard to compensate for these 'flaws' that have been thrust upon them.

For Megan, who was told she was weak throughout her childhood, emerging adulthood became a journey of proving to herself that she is strong. Those of us who get the opportunity to read her story know she is anything but weak. She clearly has a will of steel and a heart of gold. Sarah had to address the way molestation has affected and continues to affect her intimate relationship and the way she sees herself.

Megan and Sarah both experienced great struggles throughout their childhoods, but they were not broken. I'd like to share some coping mechanisms for surviving *childhood* abuse without allowing your spirit to be broken.

> **#1 Most important thing.** If you are being or have been battered, molested, sexually abused, or raped, you really need to tell someone (the police, your school psychologist or guidance counselor, or protective services). Right now. It's scary, and it may feel impossible. It is so important, though, that you seek help now if you are being abused by anyone. You do not have to stay in an unsafe situation. **It is not your fault, and you don't need to feel ashamed for experiencing abuse.** If, however, your situation is one that can't be controlled—like if your parent is being abused, but won't report or admit to the abuse, or if you are being verbally abused, please read on.

> Talk about it. Talk to someone. Find a mentor you can trust, and let it out. Tell the whole truth. Allow someone to help you process the difficult emotions that come along with witnessing or experiencing psychological and/or physical abuse. They will also be able to help you determine what kind of intervention is available.

> Know that witnessing violence and abusive dysfunction in your family is now acknowledged as a form of child abuse, and that it is hard for all witnesses, not just you. You are not weak because you are hurting or confused. You are coping in an extremely difficult atmosphere. You do not need to suffer in silence, and you certainly do not need to feel any shame.

> Follow your instincts. Sometimes when someone is belittling you or someone you love, the best thing you can do is lay low and wait it out, so as to not escalate the situation. If it feels unsafe to defend yourself in an abusive situation, don't think you're being weak for waiting it out. You're surviving.

Remind yourself that the things they are saying aren't true. Remind yourself of the beautiful things about you, even when it's hard. Never forget that your life does not have to stay this way forever. That being said, if you feel like you need to fight back or escape an imminently dangerous situation—do it. Immediately seek help. Know who your helpers are and how to get to them. That way, if this moment comes, you won't panic and not know how to get help.

- ➢ Know your escape plan, both for an emergency situation (if you're in physical danger) and your long term plan to leave the house when you're an adult. It's important for you to know that there is an end in sight, because there is, and you will make it happen.
- ➢ Be extra careful about who you date. When an abusive relationship is all you know, it is easy to slip into abusive partnerships without even realizing it just like Carrie and Megan did. Be extra diligent, and don't forget to do everything you can to build and love yourself up.
- ➢ If you have been sexually assaulted, please seek a support group specifically for sexual assault survivors. Dealing with the aftermath of sexual assault now will help you so much as you grow into your future.
- ➢ Know that you are worth it. You are worth taking care of, and you are worth holding out for something beautiful. *You are so worth it.*

One of the real difficulties of being a teen who has lived through or witnessed abuse throughout childhood is that, by now, you pretty much know it's not normal, but there's so little you can do about it. You might feel responsible for protecting the abused parent or for the situation in general. You might spend a lot of time trying to keep peace at home, trying to protect younger siblings, or trying to minimize flare-ups of anger or fighting. Between trying to manage the experience of abuse at home and the pressures of school, you don't have a lot of time to do the things everyone else is doing, like figuring yourself out. Even with all you try to do to manage, deal with, or protect yourself from the situation, you're still stuck, because you're a teenager.

As a teen in a home with domestic violence and abuse, your options are limited, but the stakes are high. Your job is to survive and to preserve and protect yourself as thoroughly as you can. The list above can help as you bide your time until you're old enough to leave and support yourself. Once you're able to leave the healing and recovery process begins, and that happens on terms that are entirely your own.

This is extremely tough. Many emerging adults, once declaring their independence from abusive families, will find themselves entirely on their own. In order to be free from abuse, they have to separate themselves from the people that usually create a support system in functional families. Like Megan, they face situations in which they are told, "Let's see how independent you are now" when a functional parent would offer support and comfort. They may have to choose between facing a difficult situation on their own or asking for help from a person they know will use their vulnerability as an opportunity to abuse or manipulate them in some way.

For this emerging adult, there are no easy choices, and it takes time and a lot of effort to create a stable life in which you are truly independent. Part of the road to healing is creating a stable life for yourself that you can thrive in, though, and it happens simultaneously with your inner healing. The more safe and stable space you create for yourself, the more room and energy you have to face your inner wounds. Being diligent is important, and even more important is knowing all along the way that you are going to make it, even when things look bleak.

You are going to make it.

One very important way to make this healing easier is to reject any further abuse from partners, friends, or family. Sometimes this happens before you realize it, but once you recognize what is happening, commit to yourself to separate from those people immediately and set good boundaries. Know your limits, and if someone crosses them, be firm and consistent in not allowing them to be in your life. Healing from childhood abuse is hard enough without allowing more abusive people into your life.

The truth about healing from abuse is that it comes from within. And it's going to hurt. Treat yourself well, and only allow others to treat you well. Then recognize this, you are going to have to fight harder to find your own truth. You will have to sift through a lot of debris left over from years of being exposed to abuse, but it is worth it.

Usually, when we quiet the outside noise (the fear, the abusers, the expectations) our own truth rises up and points us in the right direction. You might not always feel that you're getting somewhere, but every day of positive choices makes a difference. Eventually, your own voice will be louder than the fear and the pain. Life might change slowly, but following your intuition keeps it steady. With each step you take, embrace the freedom of allowing yourself be on the outside the person that you want to be on the inside.

Reflection Questions:

1. Have you or are you experiencing any abuse? Have you witnessed abuse or violence?
2. Do you know friends who have witnessed or experienced violence?
3. What do you think is/would be the worst part of experiencing or witnessing abuse?
4. Can you think of any more coping mechanisms for a teen struggling with abuse?
5. Is there any way you could support a peer who is coping with abuse?
6. Do you feel you can trust your intuition and instincts? Can you listen to your own wisdom more than the pressures from society and others?

Recovery:
Starting Over

I love Megan's story of starting over. I love her determination and perseverance. What an amazing example of strength and dignity. Like Megan shared with us at the end of her story, recovery is a lifetime commitment. It has to start somewhere, though, and motivation seems to pop up in a couple of different ways.

For some, like Megan, the motivation to drastically change things comes when a specific boundary has been crossed. When Brandon physically assaulted her, dragging her from his car, Megan cut all ties at once and changed her life drastically. It was the turning point toward the uphill climb. Think of Becca, when her dreams were being threatened and manipulated once again. That was when she'd had enough.

{A random note here: Never meet someone in a secluded area. No one. If someone wants to meet with you it should be in a well-populated public place in day time hours where you can make an easy, safe exit. Don't forget that vehicles make you isolated and portable. Meeting an ex privately is a recipe for disaster even if they're not the violent, dysfunctional type.}

For others, inspiration to change comes from getting a taste of something better; a recognition that life really could be happier. Take Carrie for example. Once she escaped her seclusion and began to experience the fun of interaction with people outside her home, it gave her the courage to leave her destructive and violent situation.

Regardless of the motivating factors, the motivation is the tipping point. When the person who is living with abuse stands up and says, "No more," and makes a decision to change their life. It is the very beginning of the work of recovery, and recovery is an uphill climb.

It involves personal healing and growth for which counseling is so helpful. It sometimes involves figuring out how to support yourself and the major life changes that go along with shifting financial needs. It involves massive changes to your children's lives if you have them, and supporting yourself while you support them.

In my experience, the recovery road is one that takes us from living in fear to living from a place of love and confidence; where we can both give and receive without fear of being abused again. In love there is empowerment, because not only do we learn to live in the world in a more loving way, we learn to love ourselves.

Learning to love ourselves after experiencing abuse or violence can be incredibly challenging. It can take many years, many more than we might think it should, to untangle ourselves from the web of false ideas we have about life, ourselves, relationships, religion, spirituality, and so much more after living with abuse for any period of time. If you grew up with abuse as a child, it is likely that there are some deeply embedded thought and behavior patterns that will need some loving care.

All of this work that we do for ourselves to recover from abuse is a fierce act of self-love and empowerment. Whether it's working through the issues abuse has left us with or creating the life we always dreamed of, it matters. Nurturing new, healthy relationships and building careers we can be proud of are concrete actions that take our power back from the people who abused us. It does not always feel this way. It's hard, we backslide sometimes, and we might become our own abusers. That's why, once we've secured ourselves from the outward threat of an abuser, we have to diligently work on ourselves—asking for help when we need it. Otherwise, the whole nightmare can start over.

The Self Work of Recovery

Before you can heal from an abusive situation, you have to separate yourself from it. This takes a good amount of gumption in and of itself. Think of Sarah slugging her creep-relative to finally make clear that she would not take his sexual assault any more—or of Megan picking up and moving across the ocean. That action created a boundary between herself and her abusive ex-boyfriend, but it still took some time for her to finally create a firm boundary between herself and her original abusers. When she cut off communicating with her father and step-mother, she made space for herself to actually heal by stating firmly to herself and her abusers that she did not deserve their incessant verbal abuse.

Self-work is an absolute necessity when we're trying to stay away from abusive situations. It's so easy to backslide, to miss the important people in your life so much that, even if they treat you badly, you go back. Some days you may even feel that they were right all along. If you are recovering from previous abuse, you can plan on spending a lot of time learning to love and honor yourself. You have to remind yourself constantly that you're lovable, you're worth it, you're smart, you're strong, etc. You have to make yourself believe it even when it feels untrue. Reminding yourself that abusers are in the business of making us believe that we are less than we are is imperative. We have to make it our business to see ourselves at our fullest potential.

We can see in Megan's story that she spent a lot of time in therapy. There is absolutely no shame in seeking help for the psychological damage that is done when we experience or witness abuse. I would suggest starting there, even, but if you're not ready for that, I would suggest starting with one of the following ideas.

> **Research.** Read about your situation. Get the statistics. Find the truth. This is helpful especially if your abuse was supported by or ignored by a social group, religion, or culture. Learning the truth behind your religion or culture can be extremely liberating. Read about domestic violence. It doesn't take long to see that you are not alone, and that there is a lot of support and encouragement out there.

➤ **Self-care.** Self-care on the outside or the inside can work wonders. I'm sure this is getting redundant, but seriously, love yourself, love your body, create a space for yourself that fills you up. It's the quickest way to build yourself up to true self-respect.

➤ **Support group.** It is so affirming to know that you're not alone, and that other people have had similar experiences. Everyone needs others to bounce ideas off of, share their stories with, and to build trust with. This doesn't need to be a formal support group geared toward abuse recovery and prevention, but it can be. If you don't like your options—you can create your own. The internet is a wonderful place to find kindred spirits (especially for introverts), since it can be easier to be vulnerable with people that you don't interact with face to face every day at first.

The self-work of recovery is really about becoming stronger every day, inside and out. As you create a life in which you are supported, both physically and emotionally, make sure you are empowering yourself practically. This can happen through education, through work that you love, through positive friendships and relationships. Whole life improvement happens because of your relationship with yourself. When you respect yourself, your standards for the way others treat you and how you treat yourself go way up. This changes everything.

Since every step toward empowerment and self-love is significant, we really need to make sure we're honoring the enormous effort it takes to make things happen. When you reach a milestone: celebrate it. When you break the habit of speaking badly about yourself: celebrate it. When you pay rent for the first time in your own space: celebrate it. When you declare independence in any little way: celebrate it. Celebrate each step toward stability and honoring your wholeness. Acknowledge those decisions for what they are: acts of empowerment. *Each and every little action is heroic.* And if all of this sounds overwhelming or not doable, think of it like this: Just do one good thing for yourself today, tomorrow, and the next day, and the day after that...

Someday the horizon will look like where you came from, because you'll already be where you've been trying to get.

Reflection Questions:

1. What's your motivation? Even if you don't need to recover from abuse, everyone needs motivation to be their best self. What's yours?
2. What are your limits? What types of behavior will you not accept?
3. Do you think you have any ideas about yourself that you think could use some tender-loving-care? Things that stand between you and self-love like, "I'm not good enough," or, "I'm too much, too intense," or, "I'm not pretty enough," etc.
4. Do you believe more of what others think about and say about you or of what you think and say about you?
5. What can you do to become stronger in yourself every day?
6. Pick three things you've done in the last month to celebrate. Nothing is too small.

Healing and Recovery as a Lifestyle

The thing about recovery from abuse is that it never really ends. Like how addicts are always in recovery from their addiction, I'm convinced that we never really "get over" the traumas we experience. We work with them, we tend our wounds, we heal, we release but we can't make our history disappear. Not to mention, life never stops hurting. Even when it's good, painful things happen. That's why we always need to be diligent in our care of ourselves. It's easy for old fears or doubts to creep in, and start to undo the good work we've done to make our lives better.

This isn't bad news, though, because recovery is all about fostering a healthy lifestyle. Eventually, living this way doesn't feel as much like work. It's just good and normal. It becomes normal to feel great and to do great things. It feels normal for people to only treat us well, and it becomes really, really abnormal and unacceptable for people to treat us badly—so abnormal that we bring the gavel down hard and quickly and then move on with our lives.

The best news is for those of you who haven't experienced abuse at all. You can implement this lifestyle into your every day challenges without having to have abusive experiences. You can take good care of yourself, set sturdy boundaries, heal your wounds (because we all have wounds, and all wounds need healing), and empower yourself every day. You can be diligent, too. You can support others, commit to awareness (living with your eyes wide open and unwilling to ignore signs of abuse in your life or other's lives), and help create a world in which there are even more people who never have to experience abuse.

The next section covers spiritual abuse and the element of fear. It also discusses how spirituality and religion can play a part in both committing acts of abuse and in one's healthy lifestyle. As we move forward into the final two sections, keep everything you've learned in mind. Notice the patterns of abuse as you read the stories, and see how those patterns make coming into adulthood even more challenging. As you read, even if you are not in abusive relationships yourself, see if you can pick up pointers from the lessons others have learned from their challenges that will smooth your way as you enter into the adult world.

{4}
Spirituality, Abuse, and Empowered Faith
Developing Your Authentic Spirit

Religion is a guiding force as well as a source of comfort, security, and encouragement for many people in the world. For some, though, sacred beliefs are the tools of manipulation. It's hard to understand why people sometimes justify their hurtful or violent behavior with their religious practices, but it happens on both large and small scales. Melanie's story gives us an inside look at what it would be like to grow up in a family in which religion played a direct role in domestic abuse.

Melanie's Story

While I was growing up, religion ruled our family life. The beliefs about family structure in that type of Christianity seemed to make domestic violence easy in our home. In the church, nearly all of the leading roles were saved for men, and the theology protected the right of men to lead their families in any way that seemed necessary to them. Or at least it was used that way.

My father was a sensitive, thinking man, and I always doubted that he seemed the abusive type to most people that I knew in the area. He was well respected by the community. I remember the fathers of some of my friends talking about their admiration for his wisdom and the way he led the family. His behavior may, even now, not be thought of as abusive by some members of the extended family or community.

My earliest memories involve my father shouting at my mother about the food she cooked, her inability to follow his directions, the lies she told, and on and on. She didn't keep the house clean enough. She didn't manage things well enough. The garden did not grow well enough. She didn't think. She must be stupid. He would go on and on about any small little mistake she made.

I would sit behind the couch in the years before I went to school while he yelled at her, soaking in all the words he said, trying so hard to imagine I was somewhere else. The rising of his voice, my mother's whimpering replies, or the loud thump of a fist on I never knew what would jerk me out of it, and I would sit and shake and sing songs to myself until the door slammed as he left for work. She would always have to take his lunch or thermos out to the truck, and the fighting would continue. I would sit there until I heard her come inside, then I would creep out just to look and make sure she was okay.

She usually didn't have any visible bruises or bleeding, but sometimes she did. She would tell me that she had hit her head on the garage door, usually. I still don't know to this day what the truth is. I only know that I, as a grown woman, have never had any such marks on my face or anywhere else for that matter. I also don't have a garage door to hit my head on.

I adored my mother. When Dad wasn't home things were usually lighthearted and cheerful. I watched my favorite cartoons, had my special toys, and probably drove Mom nuts by following her everywhere, talking her head off. Much of my childhood was really sweet, and I am grateful for the warm memories that I have. Underlying every waking moment, though, was the fear that my mom would be hurt, or that she would disappear. Not to mention the constant fear for my own safety. I always felt I was one misstep away from being hurt, myself.

I was scared to even be near my father. At bedtime, we had to give him a five, and every single night my stomach tied in knots. He would clench my hand playfully, but, tight enough to hurt. I felt like a fox in a trap every time I was near him, though he never intentionally hurt me. Admittedly, I was an extremely sensitive child, which I think intensified how I was impacted by the way things were. Even so, every night I prayed that they wouldn't fight any more, and that everyone could just be happy. It was what I wanted more than anything.

When I was small we were going to a little country church. Mom would take us every Sunday, usually teaching our Sunday School class before the regular service. There was a lot of hell fire and brimstone talk which turned into my version of the Boogie Man. It cemented the fearful life that began at home. At church, it sounded to me that God was exactly like my father. He loved me. His love was "free" but only if I did exactly as he said. Otherwise, it was hell.

The idea that devotion to God had to be more important than anything else, even life itself was made very real one night during revival week. I remember the preacher being a woman, which seems unrealistic looking back. I was so young at the time, probably around the age of 5, so this memory, while being absolutely vivid, has been played over and over so many times that's hard to know whether it's real or not. That being said, it's reflective of many such events and an ongoing message that I heard at church all throughout my childhood.

She was large, with a deep voice and seemed to me to be much more like the loud, domineering men that often came to the church than like my gentle mother. She eyed my mother from the front of the church and walked down the aisle until she was bending over her and said, "If men came here tonight with guns and threatened to kill all Christians, would you profess your belief in Jesus Christ?"

My mom answered quietly, but with sureness, "Yes."

Then the woman's eyes turned to me nestled next to mom and down the row of children sitting in the pew, "What if the gun was pointed at one of them?" The usually mostly empty church was full of the parishioners of all the area churches, our neighbors.

My mom was silent. It was terrifying, but it was something a lot of people were talking about at the time. Big time pastors had made graphic, terrifying movies about persecution and the end times, and for some reason, church people were eating it up, as though they needed a daily dose of fear to keep them prepared for the second coming of Christ.

Even though I vaguely remember a few of our neighbors coming to us after the service, disgusted at the minister for frightening us kids, I learned fear that night in a way that took decades to unlearn. The unlearning was made especially difficult by the daily reinforcement of fear that was all around throughout my childhood. By the time I left home I had my very own fear mongering voice in my head that I confused with my conscience. It frequently reminded me that we were all at risk of losing our souls to Satan. The threat was intense, imminent, and physical, and I was terrified constantly. It tainted my idea of God for many, many years.

My child's mind painted a picture, a caricature, really that melded the image of God and my father into one dark thing to be feared and obeyed without fail , but it would be many, many years before I realized what had happened. I went through my childhood losing sleep over the idea of eternity and the inescapable sin of being human, of being spanked with a belt like my siblings were, of final judgment and the rapture, of hearing my mother cry, of not being "saved" (I must have asked Jesus to come into my heart hundreds of times as a child, just to be sure), even of having to speak to my father. The religion and the family's struggle were all rolled into one mass of fear.

Part of what led me to see my dad and God as one was the fact that my dad was a lay minister during my early years. I remember the last time he preached after having fought with my mother the entire way to the church, wondering what would happen if I stood up and announced what he'd said on the way to church to the congregation. Would they still respect him? Would they still be in awe of our good behavior when they knew how we had been instructed, as always, to "act like everything is okay" upon arrival at church? My guess now is that at the time many of the other families were experiencing the same thing.

As I grew, I seemed to collect episodes in my memory. Some that stick out are the pot of vegetable soup declared too disgusting to eat that my father threw on the floor, the chicken Dad claimed was purposefully and dangerously undercooked, the fighting on the holidays (Christmas was the worst time of the year, and something dramatic always happened on Easter), and the first day of vacations which were always horrible with Dad telling Mom she had to stay home, scaring us all with the thought of our father "taking care" of us for the next week, and then allowing her to come at the last minute.....every... single... time. I don't think I can relay the intensity of these events with words. Every single time something happened it felt like the world was crashing down.

The cycle was constant, but what is so confusing looking back is that the scary upheaval isn't constant. It builds until there is a really bad episode, or there can be a random episode of mistreatment, then everything goes back to normal. People apologize and promise to do better. Everyone is "happy", until the next time. In fact, I have many, many warm and fond memories of my childhood.

As I recall, there was less physical abuse toward us kids. I was never even spanked, unlike my siblings—the reason for which I've never found. I learned from watching to be quiet, very quiet, and to always do as I was told. I can only think that I must have slipped under the radar until I was too old to be spanked. I did see spankings, which were always with my father's belt—no slight whack with a wooden spoon in our house. Spankings were almost ceremonial. There was plenty of time leading up to the big moment. This was very distressing, and the threat of being spanked was always there in the back of my mind. On one occasion I was bending over a bed waiting for my father to spank me for fighting with my brother when he abruptly told me to leave the room. My brother was spanked alone instead. The sick feeling I was left with shocked me. Even then I knew it would have been better to share the punishment, than to know that someone else was suffering when I was equally to blame.

My father was very effective with words, and his temper seemed to always get the better of him. He made it clear once I was an adolescent that he thought about as much of me as he did my mother. We seemed to have an especially testy relationship. I'd begun to challenge him about the things that went on in our home once I'd realized that things weren't right. By the time I was nine, I had told my grandmother all about it. On Father's Day, I presented him with a card that my grandmother had supported me in making. I drew pictures of the family when he was happy, and of when he was angry. The gist of the card was that it makes us all sad when you're angry, so please stop. My mom implored me to apologize, but I never did.

The worst group incidents were the family meetings that were called when things got really bad. These involved being seated around the table while my father degraded and interviewed my mother for hours. Her defense of herself was always twisted by him and used against her. Somewhere along the way I quit counting the family meetings. Most of them are blurred together in my memory so that I can't remember what was said on which occasions or what age I was at the time.

One of my father's tactics during the family meeting was to corner my mother into feeling so ashamed of herself that she would inevitably end the evening by begging our forgiveness for being such a terrible mother, which is ridiculous since she was a great mom. The patterns of blame, shame, guilt, name calling, and spiritual abuse were ever present. The consequence for any lack of submission was rage, threat, and domination, without fail.

Most of the meetings ended with my Dad deciding they had to get a divorce. Sometimes we'd be given details. For instance, most of the time we were told that Mom was moving out and we had to stay with Dad, which filled me with terror. Sometimes we were told to choose between them right then and there, being reminded that if we went with Mom, our lives would change drastically and that she had no money. We would all be forced to say out loud which parent we were choosing over and over.

Mom was always at fault for the "divorce"; her stupidity, her laziness, her dishonestly were always to blame. Dad accused her of cheating and would even weave Bible verses together in a way that would support his saying she was working for Satan, and he would coerce her to say out loud that she was working for Satan. In such a religious home, this was a traumatic thing to hear.

Additionally, Mom would have to declare all of her faults to her children; a list of the things Dad felt he had been wronged by. It was outright humiliation and manipulation. By the end we children would all be weeping, Dad would be victorious, and Mom would say goodbye to us, then they would go outside and argue some more. Sometimes he'd let her back in then. Sometimes she'd drive down the road and then come back. Only a few times was she gone for a day or more. Every time she always came back asking for forgiveness and begging to stay. When I was in junior high, my dad declared that he wasn't biblically required to forgive her anymore, since she had offended him more than seven times seventy times. Apparently he felt it was the goodness of his heart that allowed her to take care of his house, do his laundry, and cook his meals after that.

I am aware of some of the things she did that flared my dad's anger. She would lie about money from a failed business venture and she even took money out of my bank account on one occasion. I never faulted her for any of this. I know the dread of acknowledging mistakes to my father. He's unforgiving at best, torturous at worst when it comes to imperfection. No mistake is too old to bring up, and no mistake is too small to be stamped with that loathsome label: Failure.

Dad was also very controlling about money, which contributed to this financial sneaking around. Mom was always pinching pennies and stretching dollars. If we asked Dad for money, we would often get it, but only after we had fully explained to his satisfaction why we needed it. Most of the time, I was too afraid of the long, tense discussion to even ask. When mom asked him for extra money, he unfailingly accused her of being on drugs. He could not understand why the money he gave her wasn't enough for groceries, school lunches, field trips, clothes, and all the little extra expenses that having children creates.

Throughout my childhood, aside from the fighting I was constantly witnessing, there was a lot of verbal abuse directed at each of us children. As a very young child, things would be said to me that were really meant to hurt my mother. For many years after I moved out, every time I picked up a broom to sweep, or a knife to butter a piece of toast I would hear my father's voice in my ear, "Don't you know how to butter toast? Hasn't anyone ever taught you how to sweep?"

I'd come home with my straight A report card, proud as can be, only to be told that next time they should be A+'s. Frequently we were all sat at the table to write out our goals for his inspection. We were told to dream big, but in reality only certain dreams were acceptable. I never dared to speak most of my dreams out loud. I was always afraid they wouldn't be big enough. Not to mention, all creative careers seemed to unnerve him. I think he had ideas about creative temperaments and mental illness. At some point I just stopped taking my ideas seriously, too. It was very clear that only some type of mission work or work in the medical field would impress him. Being a child who desperately wanted to please him, I gravitated in those directions. Eventually, I gave up considering anything else until I was in college.

By the time I was in high school, I was so crippled by fear that I could not produce one set of goals for him. Over and over he told me, "I want to see your goals by next week." I never presented them, partly out of defiance, but mostly because I knew by then that my "goals" had been fabricated to please him and even those achievements would not please him in the end. If I said I wanted to be a doctor, he wanted me to be a surgeon, and perform mission surgeries on a boat. After a childhood of living in a mindset that was framed for his satisfaction, I couldn't even see what I really wanted in terms of a career. All I knew was that I wanted was to create a happy family in which no one was mistreated. Every career choice I made was a shot in the dark.

It was clear that he wanted greatness for me. I had always done well in school, and he wanted me to think outside of the box. What he didn't seem to realize is that to think outside of the box is an entirely personal thing. My mind was lured into another box where I learned how to satisfy, appease, and impress others. Of course, that was not sustainable, and somewhere inside I must have known it. During that last year of high school, I was laying the groundwork for my independence, but the more independent I became, the harder he fought to maintain control over me.

When Dad wasn't pushing me to fulfill his dreams for me, he was beginning to belittle me in the same ways that he did my mother. By the time I moved out of my parent's home, he had repeatedly insinuated that I was promiscuous and easy, though I was one of the most innocent girls I knew. I was told that I wouldn't amount to anything, that I had no ambition, that I was too passive, that I didn't care about anything, and worst of all, that I was weak.

These "conversations" would go on and on, sometimes, and would consist of me sitting and listening to him as he degraded me, saying things that I knew in my head were not true, wondering what in the world I was going to do to get away. If I tried leaving the room, he followed me. There was no ending the lecture until he was spent. I was valued as an intelligent, strong, insightful individual everywhere except for at home, and I knew I needed to get away.

There was a significant amount of time between the moment I realized that I needed to distance myself from my father and the moment I actually got to. Even before high school started there were moments when I was forced to see just how bad things really were.

My parents, my siblings and I took a family vacation the summer before I started high school. It was a typical vacation. A lot of arguing was happening during the build-up to leaving day. The tension was not out of the ordinary, though. There were the usual degrading comments throughout the vacation, but it was on the way home that things began to quickly unravel.

Mom and Dad were trying to decide what to do with the last day that we had before we had to start heading home. We kids went to sleep while our parents hissed at each other about it in their bed. I was sleeping at the foot of my parents' bed on the floor. In the middle of the night I woke up to the sound of my mom crying and my dad railing on about the usual things, her mismanagement of money, and basically her incapability to do anything to his standards.

I remember distinctly laying on the floor as still as I could, blood boiling, imagining clobbering him over the head with the wooden chair that was near my feet. I knew I'd never be able to move quickly enough, nor would I be able to see well enough in the dark to not hurt my mom in the process. Plus, I was pretty tiny. My body was tense as I lay there listening to him list her faults and weaknesses while she whimpered, "I'm sorry, I'm sorry."

Then, out of nowhere, I heard it; that thudding smack. It was the first time I could prove that he'd hit her, and I'd had all I could take. I leapt to my feet and shrieked, "Stop it. Stop it. Why are you doing this?"

The light switched on. I'll never forget the way my father looked at me that night. It's a look that I've seen over and over since then, as though it was only a matter of time before I realized how powerless and worthless I was.

It frightened me that night, being only about 14, and not knowing what else to do, I ran to the bathroom and cried. From the other room I heard him sort of spit out the phrase, "You'd better go tend to your daughter." And that was it; the moment I fully understood that being born female made me a disappointment, second tier, and there was nothing I could do about it. It was like he expected her to come in and tell me about the lot of being a woman, and that's basically what happened. From that night on all I could see clearly was that I had to get out.

By the spring before I graduated from high school, I was spiraling. I was pushing myself hard academically both with challenging courses and infinitely high expectations, managing constant fallout at home, and trying to pick a college. I got really sick and missed three weeks of school which knocked me from number 7 to number 9 in the top ten of our graduating class, which felt like complete failure at the time. I had hoped to improve my standing. Soon after, I hit my boiling point.

Dad had called another family meeting. I was working in the kitchen on a project for school, and told Dad I couldn't stop for the meeting. Dad accused me of not caring about the family, claiming that I should always put the welfare of the family above my studies. I had had it. All my life he had pushed me to do well in school, but when I was deeply committed to it, there was little practical support or respect from him. He'd make me go places, staying out late with the family the night before important tests, my AP exams and even the night before I took the ACT. I thrived on excelling in school. It was all I really had. These tests were investments in my future, and I felt like it was constantly under attack.

I don't remember everything that was said, but I remember telling him that he was the one who had wanted me to do well in school in the first place. I told him I wouldn't stop working on my projects because no matter what was said at the family meeting nothing was going to change because they'd been acting like this for as long as I could remember. I told my mom she should leave and be free, that I didn't think Dad would hurt us kids, and that she should go and divorce him.

Once I'd uncorked, a lot came spilling out. My father had come and stood threateningly over me, but I wasn't backing down this time. I wanted him to hit me so I could do something to actually change the situation. He didn't. I finished my project and went to bed. Things became even more heated and tense for the rest of the school year.

Eventually I graduated. My sister defended me from my Dad's insults and helped me to move out wounded, but not completely broken. She really was my strength that whole summer. When I left he told me never to come home, and not to expect any money. I knew my freedom was worth it. By that time I was learning to take his calling me stubborn and bull-headed as a compliment.

Though I'd never been allowed to have a job—my father once said I was too irresponsible even to babysit—and had no idea how to live on my own, I learned my way through being independent. I worked retail and fast food and went to school and somehow made it through that first year of college. My relationship with my parents during this time was awkward and tense. Dad would occasionally give me money, and they paid for a portion of my tuition (his threats about disowning me didn't pan out).

During that year, I'd been in a relationship that was all in all decent until after we got engaged that spring. After that we seemed to be driving each other to the edge of reason in the worst way nearly every time we saw each other. He began to say degrading things when I disagreed with him, then one night, he was trying to make me agree with his version of the truth, and I simply wouldn't when he grabbed my shoulders and slammed me against the wall repeatedly while telling me what a "pain in the ass" I was. I got away from him, but he caught me and continued to slam me against another wall. It was weird. It hurt, but not enough to leave major bruises. It was like he was trying out what it was like to manhandle someone.

I didn't see him for two weeks, and when I did, I returned his ring. If there were other warning signs that we weren't right for each other before that, and there must have been, I didn't see them, but that was enough for me. I knew then that I'd never date someone who would treat me as something to handle, or think of me as a pain in the ass again.

As time went on, I became more and more independent, though it took many years for me to set boundaries with my father to the extent I needed to for the verbal harassment to stop. My faults and failures seemed to be his favorite subjects for a while. Eventually, my struggles shifted from surviving the cycle of fear and abuse to healing from it, which has been a long, slow journey. My confidence has gradually improved, and my ability to see my own needs and desires has grown through creative expression and the support of those who love me just as I am.

I also spent a lot of time healing from the unhealthy religious aspects of my childhood and have found my spiritual way, far removed from the fear based fundamentalism I was raised with. It's so hard to communicate the impact of being around abuse as a child. I feel as though my growth was stunted, and for the last ten years, instead of living out my twenties as I "should" have, I played catch up. I've been trying to repair so that the rest of my life could be spent peacefully.

~~~~~~

Melanie's story is a complicated one, weaving spiritual, verbal, emotional, and physical abuse together in a tangled web. The roles of manipulated faith and gender inequality are present throughout, giving a firm foundation to the dysfunction in her childhood home. Here, we are going to focus on what dysfunctional faith is really about and the challenges that can come along with being female in cultures that continue to support or even celebrate gender inequality.

When Faith is Used as a Weapon
And What it's Really About

Faith, spirituality, and religion are such personal, intimate and important matters, that when one feels their faith system has been attacked the immediate response is to go on the defense—to protect what is theirs. In no way am I setting out to attack religion. I hold religion in the highest regard, and am a diligent tender of my own personal faith. I staunchly believe religion should be protected from those who seek to use it for control and personal power, which is what happened in Melanie's story. If there is to be any wagon circling, let's circle our wagons against those who would use religion maliciously.

Melanie's story is unique in this book in that her family's belief system was used so directly for control and to justify her father's abusive behavior. The fear she felt at home was reinforced at church, and some of the core ideas she learned at church were used at home to justify abuse. I think most would agree that religion, at its purest, does not support abusive behavior. Unfortunately, though, it has been used (and still is today) to support the subjugation of populations based solely on their race, social class, gender, and sexuality. Here, we are focusing on the suppression of women and children.

Melanie's story isn't the first time the issue of the misuse of faith has come up in our stories. Think about Carrie, whose boyfriend who used her guilt over sex to call her a whore and further control her. Think of Becca, who experienced overwhelming guilt over leaving her abusive husband and filing for divorce until some wonderful ladies taught her that God would never want her to stay in an abusive situation. I know far too many people personally who are staying in abusive relationships right now because of their faith organization, or because ministers tell them it's sinful to leave. I often wonder why there are exceptions that make abuse more acceptable than divorce. These kinds of beliefs are what convince me that some cultures are set up to keep women under control through fear, not always of violence, but of disappointing God. It is a well-functioning tool. It is also a symptom of an organization that has bankrupt its integrity.

When faith, in particular, is used as a weapon, or as the means to control, it reaches down deep to the spirit and grows from there. Spiritual leaders, such as ministers, have an enormous amount of influence over people of faith. They are trusted, looked to for advice, are considered to be authorities on God, and are basically thought of as beacons of wisdom. While I've known plenty of beautiful, good-hearted ministers, I've also known some who were all too eager to embrace the power that comes with the position. It's important to be careful, and to realize that they are just human beings who have no more access to God than you. They don't have any magic answers, and they are just as likely to be abusers as anyone else.

A religious leader who is leading their community with fear is engaging in spiritual abuse. A religious leader who defends an abuser is empowering abuse with their religious authority, and that, too, is spiritual abuse. A religious leader who disempowers an abused person, or places blame on an abused person who comes to them for help is engaging in spiritual abuse.

A teacher of true faith won't engage in any such behavior. True faith does not need to guide or manipulate your behavior through fear or disempowerment. True faith guides you toward courage. Fear has no place in the formula of faith. If fear is present, then it's not real faith, it is control, which, as we have seen, is a part of the abuse family.

Fear is a powerful weapon no matter who or what it is wielded by. Whether you are fearful of immediate physical injury, of an eternity in hell, both, or something entirely different, the fear itself is what does the damage. It leaves you feeling unsure of everything and everyone, especially of yourself. Melanie never knew a life without fear. Even her earliest memories are steeped in fear of her father and of God.

117

It's easy to see how, when constantly being reminded of God's wrath (or of God's support of her father's wrath), the messages of forgiveness, loving-kindness, self-discipline, justice, charity, and renewal, the true roots of Melanie's religion, would be difficult to fully understand or trust. They would have to be excavated from the rubble of control and fear—a tall task to ask of a child. In Melanie's situation, the fear became crippling. She learned early to hide behind the couch, to be silent and still to slip under the radar. Perhaps because of this, it wasn't until she was heading toward independence that she was directly verbally abused.

As wonderful as it is that Melanie escaped without being physically abused, her silence and stillness couldn't protect her from the penetrating fear that was a constant in her environment. As she said, "Underlying every waking moment, though, was the fear that my mom would be hurt, or that she would disappear. Not to mention the constant fear for my own safety. I always felt I was one misstep away from being hurt, myself."

You can imagine what living with that kind of fear would do to a child. People of all ages can be crippled by fear, and that's what the manipulation of faith in order to control another human being is about. It's a powerful tactic used by those who abuse to weaken those they want to keep under their thumb.

Religion doesn't have to be the source of this kind of institutionally supported fear. Think of Carrie and her police officer husband. He used his position to frighten her and make her feel powerless. It doesn't take an institution's support to inflict others with fear, either. Megan's father used violence and a weapon. Sarah was frightened that her abuser, a friend of the family, would harm her more invasively if she told or fought back.

Regardless of the source of fear, it has the power to make us feel less capable, less whole, less worthy, and ganged up against. It can silence our voice. It can make us think our abuser has all the cards and we're all alone and powerless. It causes us to tiptoe through our lives and around the more explosive people and situations in them.

118

When we live in fear, we tread carefully. We make decisions based on what will cause the least amount of disturbance to the person we're afraid of (or the ideas they left us with). This exacting care isn't taken out of mindfulness, but out of the fear that one wrong step will bring the safety we've carefully constructed crashing down around us.

Fear doesn't have to be so "big" to play a big role in our lives. Little fears that don't seem to matter can make a huge impact on how we approach life, too. Because, while our innate fear responses play a good and significant role in keeping us safe in emergency situations, they can also keep us from realizing our full potential when they're kept in overdrive during our everyday moments.

It's important to take a look at our attitudes about fear, and to figure out where fear is playing a restrictive role in our lives so we can stop tiptoeing around it. We need to be masters of our fear instead of letting it master us. Chronic fears, the kind we're constantly tiptoeing around, are like cobwebs woven by our own misperceptions of ourselves. They only serve to darken our lives. If we spend some time seeking out the cobwebs so we can deal with them head on, we're less likely to run into them when we're not expecting to. When we clear out our fears, we make room for empowered, authentic faith and action. This is a fierce way to protect our spiritual and mental health.

Checking in with Ourselves
A Walk through the Shadows

Throughout most of this book I've focused on building up our lives through taking good care of ourselves and setting solid boundaries. Sometimes, though, we run into roadblocks. Sometimes, it can feel like no matter how hard you try you can't get to goodness. Perhaps you've been trying many different ways to make a specific goal a reality, or to make an important decision that you just can't figure out. If you feel like you're running into walls over and over, or like you're struggling through mud then it's time for a walk through the shadows.

Whenever you feel like you need to, it's a wonderful thing to get real with yourself about the things within you that are holding you back. What are you afraid of? Do you have any beliefs about life or yourself that are tripping you up? These beliefs tend to boil down to unexamined fears, and most often, the things we're afraid of only seem so scary because we're seeing them in shadow instead of full light.

One of the issues with fear is that sometimes things seem so scary that we seek comfort and security in things that aren't helping us to release our fears and may even perpetuate them—like a person who is afraid that they aren't lovable so they settle for an unhealthy relationship to keep from being lonely. There is nothing wrong with seeking comfort and security. Comfort and security are very good, restorative things, but only when they come from healthy places that serve our highest good. Facing our fears is also a good thing. It's a kind of deep cleaning.

Checking in with yourself to clean out those cobwebby fears is pretty simple. Say there is something you've always desperately wanted to do, but you've never done it. Ask yourself why, and then watch for the real answers, no matter how uncomfortable those answers make you feel. Maybe there is something you know you're afraid to do or even think about. Ask yourself why, and then be willing to hear the real answers. Maybe there is something you do because you've always done it that way. Ask yourself why. Maybe you've always thought a certain something about yourself. Ask yourself why. Ask yourself if it's really true.

Seeing a theme here? Asking yourself why, and then giving yourself permission to answer honestly is such a great way to see the difference between the things you do because they reflect your true self and who you want to be and the things you do and think because someone has told you to. In this category is where you may find some fears lurking around.

Sometimes fears show up as negative beliefs about yourself. Maybe you think you're ugly, fat, boring, stupid, too loud, or too shy. Those kinds of ideas that we carry about ourselves are usually coupled with fears like, "If I'm ugly and fat, then no one will want to be my friend or partner, so I'll always be lonely," or, "If I'm boring, then I'm never going to fit in anywhere," or, "If I'm stupid I'm not going to get into college and my whole life is going to be a failure," or, "If I'm shy people will think I'm weird and make fun of me." Maybe you even have a whole list of examples of why your beliefs and fears are true.

Acknowledging the fears can be really hard. We want to pack them up tightly and put them away where we won't have to deal with them. We may want to pretend they don't exist. But even from their box in the corner they're still impacting the way we feel about ourselves. Instead of stuffing them away, let's get them out and sit with them. Let's name them. Let's get to know where they came from and why we think what we think about ourselves.

Write it out. Draw it out. Chart it out. Dance it out. Whatever. See what you think of yourself on paper. See if you can follow your memories back to when, where, and how these ideas formed. How old were you? What was happening in your life? Bring as much as you can out of your mind and onto the page where you can see it and think about it rationally. Doing so shines a light on your fears in a powerful way. Sharing your fears with a trusted friend or mentor is courageous. Getting help from a counselor around these issues is a fierce act of self-care.

Just so you know, we're not doing this to torture ourselves, or to wallow in our own shadows. Rather, we do this because fears create roadblocks that get in the way, making it difficult or even impossible for us to get to where and who we want to be. They also take up valuable space in our lives that we could be using to create more beauty, because that's what we get to do when we're finished cleaning up the shadows that are stopping us.

The thing about fears is that when we bring the light to them, say, "I see you," and choose to build beauty in their presence, they gradually cease to be scary. It's challenging at first, but once you work your fear-facing muscle, it begins to feel more like an adventure than a nightmare. If you can be brave enough to see what you fear most, you can take back your power, harness it, and start steering your course free from the crippling influence of chronic fear. *Resource :: Tara Wagner (theorganicsister.com) is a life coach that I've worked with. She developed a program called Digging Deep. If you need help getting to the bottom of your fears and personal roadblocks, Digging Deep could be a great tool for you. {Unpaid promo here. I just love Tara.}*

Trading Fear for Freedom

Fears are only powerful when we allow them to be. One of the ways we allow fears to have far too much influence over us is when we try to ignore them. So often, fears are tiptoed around like a sleeping dragon. When we choose to live this way, we can't operate at full volume, speed, or freedom. The trick here is to realize that when operating at full volume, speed, and freedom, we've got what it takes to tame the dragon. We already have what it takes to conquer our own fears, if we choose to acknowledge and use our personal power.

There's an inverse relationship between our fears and our personal power. When we exercise our personal power and freedom, fears diminish. However, personal fears can make exercising power and freedom feel impossible or useless. The good thing about this is that it's fairly easy to tip the scale in our favor. One action that embraces our personal power can act as a catalyst for rousing our courage.

Finding and facing your fears can certainly be a daunting task, and may involve revisiting past trauma. Once you've uncovered your fears, though, processing that fear and making space in your life for goodness doesn't have to be heavy. Any approach that works for you will do. Humor, creative expression (writing, drawing, dance, gardening, anything), gathering knowledge, creating external atmospheres that reflect the way you want to feel inside. Anything that helps you to feel more sturdy and steady in the presence of your fear: do that.

The goal is not to beat the fear away as much as it is to shed light on the dragon, and create beauty in its presence. Sit with it. Understand it. There are times when one solid glimpse at a fear is enough to make it vanish, more often than not, though, it takes patience and persistence to learn to take your power back. Above all, trust yourself. You have what it takes to sweep this fear out of your life. Follow your intuition. Trust the ideas that pop into your head. Work with them and see what happens. If one idea is a dud, no worries, something else will come up.

However you choose to deal with the fear, the important thing is to keep an eye on the way that you're feeling, because your feelings are a good indicator of your needs. If it's a really big fear that you're working with, like Melanie's God/Dad fear, there may be times when it feels like it's closing in on you. If you're getting to a place where the work you're doing to process the fear is giving you more anxiety than it's processing, it's time to take a break. Go for a walk. Read a light book. Do something simple that you love and that gives your mind a rest. This isn't a sprint, it's more of a marathon, so take your time and remind yourself that cleaning out fear is really big and valuable work that both you and everyone around you is going to benefit from. It's okay if it takes a long time. And don't forget, it's *always* okay to ask for support.

There comes a point when you realize that you don't need to process the fear any more. You understand it thoroughly and you've built yourself up in its presence. All that's left to do is let go. This isn't always as easy as it seems it should be. For whatever reason, sometimes we grow fond of our fears. Sometimes they feel like comfort; like a part of ourselves. Sometimes hiding behind the fear seems like a much better idea than letting it go and standing in your own strength. Please know that we all deal with this, and that you don't have to let every single thing go, and you certainly don't have to let everything go at once.

When you get to the point where you know you've exhausted any work you can do with a fear, just trust yourself to know what's best for you. What is important is the work you've done to build yourself up in the presence of the fear. There will come a time when it feels natural to let it go. Sometimes it's right away, and sometimes it's five years later. Every little thing you do to empower yourself in the presence of your fear creates more space in your life for goodness. It liberates you a little bit more, and then when you're ready for it, freedom is on the other side of letting go.

Once you get used to it, taking walks through your shadow side becomes a cherished practice. Eventually we acknowledge that what we see as weaknesses, the things that make us afraid about ourselves and about the world are simply shadows, and shadows are always present. The fact that negativity, fear, trouble, and struggle exist is just part of being alive. I do believe the scale tips in favor of the positive, and that the majority of our time can be spent focusing on the lighter, brighter side of life. It's important to know, though, that this world of ours does not have to be perfect to be good, and we don't have to be perfect in it to have a beautiful life. It is okay to acknowledge the things within us and around us that are not perfect, and have peace about them. Not everything has to be worked on. Only the things that are specifically stopping us from making the progress we want to make need to be sorted out.

It seems to me that when we have fears, like the fear that we are unlovable or that we'll never succeed, or that the world won't accept us as we are, it's because we've bought into the idea of a perfection that we don't measure up to. Society gives us the idea that we can buy or create perfection and that the only way to belong is to fit in with some external standard of perfection. But no one measures up to the standards of perfection.

Instead of trying to measure up to unattainable standards of perfection, we can get to know ourselves better. We can ask ourselves what causes our own fears. We can take a look at how we really feel about ourselves. We can get more comfortable with the things that we find embarrassing about ourselves. We can learn to love ourselves as we are. Shadows and all.

When we are able to let go of our fears of not being perfect, not measuring up, not being able to make it and instead learn to trust ourselves, learn to say, "I can handle this," when we run into a challenge and believe that we can, we find ourselves free.

Reflection Exercise:

Take some time to think about a fear you have about yourself or your life. First: figure out what it is. If nothing comes to your head right away, maybe start with an idea that you have about yourself that makes your life worse, like I'm not pretty enough, or I'm not smart enough. Ask yourself why until you've figured out what fear is hiding underneath that idea. Write it out if that helps. Let it wander through the back of your mind for as long as you need to. Once you've figured it out just sit with it. Acknowledge that it's there. Once you've gotten comfortable with acknowledging it, then start thinking of ways to manage your fear. Most fears are liars, so maybe you could start there, by acknowledging that it's not true, then build your way up from there. Ask yourself, "If it's not true, but I still believe it, what can I do to change that? How can I teach myself to believe the truth?" Then act on it. Trust your instincts and believe that you can figure it out. This could take anywhere from minutes to months. Just roll with it.

Being Female
And When it Feels Less Than Awesome

Aside from fear, Melanie's story says a lot about how not all female children are valued as equal. Even now, when women are generally considered to be liberated. For Melanie, being a girl wasn't that awesome. She believed by the time she went to high school that she would always be a disappointment to her father because she was female. Also, the fact that she was female led to her father treating her in a manner similar to his treatment of her mother. Melanie was simultaneously disempowered and pushed toward achievement.

Being a female can be complicated. Even when your family is in favor of equality there is still a lack of balance in the world, and it creates a lot of confusion and real struggle that reveals itself more and more as your womanhood unfolds. In the present, girls can be whatever they want to be, feminine, tough, creative, intelligent, loud, ambitious, you name it, and that is a very good thing. The thing is that we've gotten to a place where women can be so much that sometimes we feel that we have to be it all at once so that we can be regarded as equal. I'm not sure that was the goal of women's liberation, though. In fact, I'm convinced that it was not the goal at all. The goal was and is that we are free to *make choices; be who we want to be.*

Because we are innately worthy, there is no reason why a woman should not be able to create any experience in her life. Realistically speaking, some experiences don't fit together in a way that makes for happiness for everyone, though. If you find yourself wanting a life full of everything, you can make it happen, just maybe not all at once. Just like you can only be on so many sports or academic teams each season before you get burnt out, you can only fill so many roles at once. And women have a lot of roles to choose from. Daughter, student, coach, friend, employee, employer, adventurer, mother, wife, entrepreneur, sister, volunteer, mentor, activist, and on and on it goes. It's all too easy to over commit.

You can only do so much at once and still do it well, and there is nothing wrong with that. Let me say that again: You can only do so much at once and still do it well, and there is nothing wrong with that. Nothing at all. As women today, we get to choose which roles we want to play and when. It's important to choose carefully, because certain roles are overbearing and they don't share life space well.

Unfortunately, almost everywhere, it is still considered okay for people to stand and toss roles at others (subtly or not) through pressure and expectation, which is what happened to Melanie. Her father pressured her to perfect her studies, be a submissive daughter—which included being available for and submissive to ongoing psychological abuse, and to choose a career that would impress him. The religious culture around her pressured her to adhere to a moral code without question, and created a very specific and limited role for women.

Being female doesn't feel so great when you have another person, or a society bearing down on you, fitting you with roles that you never chose. So let me say this: You don't have to be a mother or a wife if that's not what you want, and you don't have to be a career woman if that's not what you want. You don't have to fill any roles at all. You may have to develop some hunter-gatherer skills, but the point is that external expectations, particularly the ones that define femininity in a narrow way, can make being female feel like a strain, or even worse, a hindrance.

The truth is that no one gets to define femininity for you. Not now. Not when you're 30. Not when you're 80. Not ever. You define it for yourself. You decide which roles you want to fill and for how long. You decide which roles fit together in your life and which don't. You can spend your life switching roles or you can fill the same role your whole life long. The point is, women are liberated today because we have the freedom to choose. We have our hardcore

127

feminist ancestors to thank for that. I think the last thing they would want is to see women suffering in a new way—suffocating under all those roles that other people think they should be filling.

The truth is that you can do whatever you want with your life. It's just a ton of work. Building on your strengths and your assets is a good idea, but honestly, you can create the life you want from scratch one step at a time if you're willing to work, and I mean *work* for it. Just remember to try to be realistic about your expectations, and really think about how you plan to fit your responsibilities and roles together (don't forget to leave enough space for you to take good care of yourself and have some fun along the way).

Being female really is amazing. We have so much opportunity and so much freedom to explore both our inner and outer worlds. If you're feeling less than awesome about your femininity, maybe take a look at how many roles you're playing and how many of those you chose and how many were chosen for you by people in your life or through societal pressure. You deserve to have the life you want and you can start building it right now. It's what being an empowered woman is all about.

Reflection Questions:

1. What roles do you play?
2. Did you choose them for yourself? Do you chose how you fill them? Do you enjoy them?
3. What are your plans for the future?
4. How can you experience everything you hope to experience in life?
5. What can you start with?

Empowered Faith

Melanie's negative experiences with religion were disempowering and debilitating in many ways. Religion contributed to the ground that abuse and fear grew out of for her, but her experience does not define the potential of faith. Faith that we have chosen for ourselves, that has grown up through us, and is ingrained in our life gives us solid footing. In its pure form, faith is a powerful antidote for fear, and an able healer of abuse related wounds.

Faith shows us how to face and carry our burdens with power and grace, and gives us the peace of not carrying them alone. True faith can be found within the organization we were born into, one of our own choosing, or none at all. Some people, like Melanie, have to take a step back from the organization they were born into to find their authentic faith, but not everyone has so extreme an experience.

Empowered faith is the faith that has grown authentically in you; it's the faith you choose to tend—the way you choose to tend it. Faithful practice should be something we get to lean into, and something that pushes us to grow. It should never be something that causes us to feel afraid, or that we're not good enough, unworthy of love, or at an accelerated risk of danger in this life or after it. It also should not make us feel superior to others.

True faith is not about fitting into a set of rules. Religion is about practicing a way of life that brings us into alignment with what is Sacred. This Sacredness goes by many different names. This truth is accessible in as many different ways as there are human beings on earth. It is manifested on earth through our relationships with God, ourselves, and with others. Worthy practices won't be *afraid* of other paths of faith or non-faith, education or deep thinking, and they won't be afraid to have their theologies questioned. Worthy, healthy faith practices have no need for these fears or any others. Worthy practices do not squabble with other practices over who is right, wrong, or better. Respectfully disagreeing is enough, as is, sometimes, a simple nod of acknowledgement. Sometimes people of faith must love each other from a distance, if it's the best we can do.

Empowered faith is only really possible when there is freedom to question and grow within the practice. If difference is treated as deviance in a faith community, then it is a community of fear and control rather than healing and growth. Fortunately, since the comfort of a faith family is important to many people; many, many faith communities do leave room for personal differences and experiences.

Most often, the loudest, most insistent religious voices don't represent the majority, and we should never forget that faith is in the ownership of each individual. This means that how we understand the concept of God is something that happens within us, and no group of leaders or faction of a religion should have the power to define and judge everyone else's practice.

If you find that your faith is entrenched in a lot of fear, or that your questions about your faith are met with anger or absolutism, please know that God is so much bigger than fear. People may be afraid of your doubt, or of the way you express your spirituality. People may lash out against you out of fear. But God is not afraid. God is simply there. Begin with compassion, treating others the way you wish to be treated, which is at the center of all major world traditions, and God will meet you there.

Reflection Questions:

1. What are your thoughts on faith and freedom?
2. Do you feel you've chosen your own faith?
3. Do you think faith supports us or ensnares us? Neither? Both? Why?
4. How can you protect your spirituality from abusive people and cultures?

Standing Your Ground

Emerging into Adulthood

With Grace and Assurance

In all of the stories that have been shared here in which relationship abuse occurred, we can see the consistency of girls who, while stepping into womanhood, got sidetracked in an abusive relationship or in the need to invest in deep healing from abusive childhood experiences. The final story reflects a different sort of manipulative situation in which a young woman was not free to steer her own course and suffered greatly along the way for it. Following her story we'll dig into what it takes to emerge boldly and gracefully into adulthood.

Lauren's Story

Lauren's story involves being controlled and manipulated by her family as a young adult. Her parents' extreme strictness during childhood evolved into an unhealthy involvement in their adult children's lives. When Lauren chose to date a person of Hispanic origin against their approval, her family reacted by giving her an ultimatum: choose him or us. The situation escalated when she became pregnant.

Here's a transcript of our discussion that has been edited for clarity:

Lauren: I mean, I was an adult. I had Mindy when I was 21, but it didn't start with my pregnancy...

Rob and I met at my sister's wedding. When they found out he was Hispanic, my parents told me I could be friends with him, but that was all. Of course, I found him attractive, and wanted to date him all the more because they were telling me not to. We started dating at college. Eventually, my parents found out and weren't happy about it at all.

Midway through the semester the college kept notifying me that my payment was past due for the next semester's tuition. Both of my parents lied to me about it, trying to put me off. Then finally they broke down and told me the truth. They were sending me to another school. Dad told me that over break he was going to have Mom take me up to school to go through my things and pack. I told him I'd pack it myself. Then I decided they weren't going to tell me I couldn't go to school there or that they're sending me somewhere else. When I told them that over Christmas break, they said they wouldn't pay for it. I said that was fine, there are lots of kids who have to pay for their own school and I was sure I could find a way to do it.

I was talking to Rob on the phone in my bedroom at my parents' house, and Mom came in and started yelling at me. She called me a slut. Then a few minutes later, they came in together and told me I needed to pack some things. Dad was taking me to a hotel because Mom was freaking out. He needed me to think some things over for a couple of days. I packed a suitcase and a plastic tub of stuff.

He left me at the hotel saying I was going to stay there for a couple of days to think about whether I was going to stay with them or go with Rob. He told me that if I moved back to my school and got back with Rob I couldn't ever stay with them at home again. I was crying and freaking out. I stayed one night and called Rob. He drove up from his hometown to come get me. I pocketed the rest of the money Dad had left for the hotel stay, and I left with Rob.

I ended up having to go figure out financial aid and get a job before the next semester started. I had to get my parents to say in writing that they weren't paying for anything anymore so I could be an independent. I worked for the Bursar's office.

That summer, my mom showed up at our apartment where I was living with Rob and two other guys. It was storming, and she said, "You have to get dressed and come with me." She drove me around the city trying to convince me to move home and leave Rob. She even tried to use our pets to get me to come home. She said the animals missed me. I told her it was uncalled for and that I was an adult. She had just shown up. That's how desperate she felt, I guess. They were upset now that we were having sex and living together out of wedlock, but before that they were just mad that he was Hispanic.

We were going to elope. We went to get my birth certificate, and we were going to Mexico. When we got to the Health Department I said, "I can't do this." I knew I couldn't marry him. Then I thought— if you don't love him enough to marry him, why are you with him? I left my family for him, so I wasn't just having fun, but I just couldn't marry him and leave them permanently. I went and stayed with a friend in town for a couple of days then I called my parents. They were okay about it. I think they were just happy that I didn't run away with him. They wanted me to come back home and pretty much weren't going to have anything to do with me ever again, they made it clear, if I stayed with him, because he's Hispanic.

I moved home two weeks after I'd broken up with Rob. He'd asked me to take a pregnancy test, and I did. It came back negative. I moved back home and I started getting morning sickness. I took another test which came back positive. The first person I told was a friend's mom, because I couldn't tell Mom and Dad. She originally agreed to tell them, but then decided that I should be the one to tell them. I drug it out for a few days then finally told them while we were talking about me going back to school at the local community college. When I told them, they just went silent.

I thought my mom would yell, but she was just silent. You know my mom's angry when she doesn't talk at all. They asked me if I was going to have an abortion. I said no. Then Dad said, "I guess we'll have to get you to a doctor to make sure everything's okay." When they asked if I was going to keep the baby, I said I'd like to, but they were all, "Well that would be selfish," and then we had that whole discussion.

I decided to go back to school, still, which was probably a bad idea with all the emotions going on. I felt sick and tired all the time. I was pregnant with someone's baby who I still had feelings for. The fights I'd had with my parents before had worn me down, and it was all just too much.

When I was pregnant and in school Rob would drive to see me, or I would drive to my old school to see him. Then my mom started tracking the miles and realized I was going somewhere other than school. They literally did the math to figure out that I was driving to my old school. They told me if they found out I was going there they would kick me out.

My sister wouldn't speak to me, and Mom wouldn't talk to me about the pregnancy. I had no clue what was going on. This was the first time I'd been pregnant. My dad would crack jokes every once in a while, but that's all that was said.

Then they started keeping me inside. I wasn't allowed to go out in public. Literally. I wasn't allowed to go anywhere with anyone. Everyone already knew, though. It's a small town. Everyone knows everything about everyone, especially if you don't want them to. At one time my mom brought up the idea of sending me to Texas to live with a friend of the family. My mom has a very old fashioned sense of thought. There wasn't a boarding house to send me anymore, so she wanted to ship me as far away as she could. Fortunately, my dad stepped in and said, "Absolutely not. Are you kidding me?"

Mom drove me to all my appointments. She wasn't nice to me during the process, so I didn't trust her to come back to the room during the check-ups. I can understand why she wasn't happy about the situation, but if she was going to keep me living in her home, at least treat me a little nicer. If they didn't want me there, they shouldn't have had me there. Instead, they told me, "If you keep the baby, we'll have nothing to do with you. You don't have a job. You don't have a car. You'll just moved back here. You're going to live on welfare. You'll end up shacking with some guy to raise your kid and then you'll end up having more kids with him." They went on and on. And I didn't have a job, or a car, or know anyone who'd help me. I didn't know how to go about all this any other way but theirs. They knew everyone in town. If I did anything, they'd find out about it anyway.

"If you stay," they said, "which is the least selfish thing you could do, we'll continue to pay for your school. You can continue to live here, and you'll get a job after you graduate."

They really hit me hard, especially my dad, with the idea that it would be selfish to keep the baby. So I decided to give the baby up. Well, then they told me I couldn't tell Rob I was pregnant, because the law was that if the Dad doesn't know about the child before it's adopted, he still can't try to get rights or custody after the child has been adopted out. I had already told him, though. He had the right to know that I was pregnant with his child. He ended up signing the papers, too.

When he and his father were trying to make me feel really guilty about giving Lily up for adoption, I would remind them that Rob signed the papers, too. His dad really wanted me to feel guilty and horrible for it, and of course I did, because how do you give up your first born child? Even if you're trying to convince yourself it's the least selfish thing to do, it's still your child.

Later into the pregnancy, they started giving me couples to pick from. I did and didn't get to pick who was adopting my child. They went through the church and found some type of website of Christian couples trying to adopt. They had a file of a few couples for me to choose from. The couple I chose had tried for a long time to have a baby, weren't rich, and weren't trying to "buy" a baby. They did reimburse medical bills, and I did meet them and their attorney. I went to the hospital of their choice for all of my check-ups.

I think only a mother who has carried a child and has gone through that whole experience really understands what giving up a baby would feel like. When I had her in the hospital, mom was in the room, and I found out I'd had a girl. They asked me if I wanted her in the room with me, if I wanted to feed her and change her diaper, and I said yes. My mom said, "I don't think that's a good idea."

I said, "I carried her for nine, almost ten months, and I'm giving her up for adoption in two days. If I want to feed her and change her diaper, I'm going to. You're getting your way. I'm giving her up—that's what you wanted, so at least let me have this."

When my parents came up to visit, they wouldn't hold her, but they saw her, even my sister saw her. It was Mother's Day weekend when I left the hospital, and they took me out to dinner. So everywhere it's babies and little kids and I'm thinking, "*Why would you take me out on Mother's Day weekend?*" It was ridiculous.

After I gave her up for adoption, I kind of sulked around the house, because I was really upset. Mom told me I had to get a job and I couldn't just lay around all day. I started working at a deli. I worked there for a few months, then they sent me to a school that I didn't get to pick. They sent me to a really conservative Christian school, and I only stayed there for a semester.

Rob and I started sneaking around to see each other again. Mom didn't know for a while. At that point I was going through a rebellion phase. I was just thinking, "*Screw it. I don't want to go to this college with all these goody goodies, and I don't want to listen to all this church talk with this big secret I have.*"

A lot of the girls there were just looking for a really churchy guy to marry, but that's not what I was looking for. I was being forced to go there and it just really pissed me off. You couldn't have rated R movies, if you were dressed too revealingly—tight pants, too much flesh, anything—they made you go back and change. It was just a weird, bad experience. Then after I came back from Thanksgiving break, I started getting really tired. I was sleeping through all my classes. I couldn't get out of bed. I'd get up to go eat, that's it. Rob came and got me and took me to my old school, and I took a test. There it was, the faintest little line.

Mom called me when she got a change of address card in the mail, and that's when I told her, "Yeah, I'm not coming back home." She lost it, and wanted to know what I was doing. I told her I was going back to my old school. I didn't tell them I was pregnant until I was already six months along. Then I got a letter from them asking me why I was having this baby. I kept reading it trying to figure out if they were telling me they wanted me to have an abortion.

I was scared shitless. I'd been pissed off and reckless. I wasn't having a baby to fill some void. My first thought was *I hope it's not a girl, because that would just remind me more of Lily.* At this point, it was too late. Rob's dad and cousin were trying to convince Rob to convince me to have an abortion. His dad told him I was irresponsible.

While I was pregnant I was working two jobs and going to school. Rob was just going to school. After I had Noah, I got a better job at a restaurant and continued to work and go to school. Rob refused to work. He was upset that I was working all the time, but I told him someone had to pay the bills. He didn't have to pay rent or anything, but he racked up a huge credit card bill, and didn't tell me he wasn't paying for it.

A few months after Noah was born I moved into another apartment. He was going to finish out his lease then move back in with us. The new apartment was going to be under my name instead of his. Then he decided that he didn't want to move in because he needed his study space and the other apartment, and we could just trade Noah off every other week or every couple of days so he could study.

I told him I was going to school and working, too. This is my child. I don't just pawn him off. You make time to study whether it's when he's in bed, or when he's playing. Rob said he cried too much, but he was a really good baby. He didn't cry that much. He slept through the night. I would put him in his car seat and do my homework. He always wanted to be in his car seat and he would play with toys. As a baby, he was fine. He could entertain himself. He didn't need me to hold him all the time or anything and I'd do homework or I'd wait till he went to bed, or I'd do it in between classes. Basically, Rob was full of shit. Welcome to parenthood and adulthood. Apparently he wasn't ready for it.

Even so, I stayed with him. He would stay nights at my place, he just wouldn't give up his other place. I started to think, *"This is weird. You won't give up your apartment to be with us but we're still together?"* Finally I'd had it. He wasn't paying for anything. I got so mad one time that he went out and got a diaper bag and a pack of diapers. He got them free from a friend. That was all he contributed to his child. I got really mad and said, "You don't work. You don't do anything. You don't pay anything for the baby. You're lucky you don't have to pay rent."

He'd pull that whole, "Well, school is my career." Well, this is your child. It got to the point with Rob where I was comfortable with him, but I didn't love him. We shouldn't have gotten back together even after I found out I was pregnant. I was still being rebellious. It was my chance to get away from the school I didn't want to be at and my family. Then I moved in with him, but there was nothing romantic about our relationship. It wasn't great. We weren't excited about having a baby together. I was working all the time and going to school and he goes to school and complains he's tired and busy. It was just very stressful.

We were fighting a lot. There was one time that Rob came at me and I shrunk down against the wall. He didn't have his fist raised, but he was shouting at me, which he'd never done. I just remember thinking it was going to be the first time and it might not end well. I've never been hit by anyone. He said, "I'm not going to hit you, if that's what you're thinking. What are you doing? Did you think I was going to hit you? I would never do that."

"Well," I said, "You're coming at me pretty aggressively."

Finally I reached my breaking point with him because I just thought, "*How long are you going to stay with this just because you're comfortable and you don't know anything else? It was hard enough leaving your family, but now you're going to go off completely on your own? What's that going to be like?*"

Now I was going to be totally alone. Finally I went out and I bought a car, and eventually left him. I realized I could do things on my own and I didn't need to lean on the idea of someone to lean on.

After I ended the relationship there were times when Rob didn't come to see Noah at all. The whole first summer he didn't have him at all. Then he'd complain because I would prompt him to come. But Noah needed to see his dad. Rob eventually moved out of the country. I can't imagine living that far away from my child and not calling every day. He blames it on his job. He could work around that, but his career is the most important thing to him.

For a while I was taking Noah to Mom and Dad's church every week. I was trying to stay close to them, and to trying to get my sister to be a part of my life again. She stopped coming over for Sunday dinner because I was there. At one point I tried to give her Noah's baby clothes for her son, but she wouldn't accept them. She went off about how she doesn't want people who would not be a good influence around her child, and if we met on the street she'd have nothing to do with me since we have nothing in common. She said I'd made a bad name for the family, and that I was an embarrassment to her at work. I was sobbing. Nothing I could do would get me back into her good graces; even if I was driving over an hour to go to church with them every week. For a long time I really struggled with that, because this is my sister. These are the relatives I'm going to have after my parents die. I got to the point where I had to let it go.

Mom tells me I should get back ahold of her, but I've tried. I send cards and letters, I email, I call. She won't respond. She'll have nothing to do with me and I'm done. I'm done staying up and worrying about it – wondering what I can do. There's nothing I can do. I'm done begging for forgiveness. And for what? I don't know what I've done to wrong *her*. She's my sister and I love her, but there's only so much I can do.

At least Mom and Dad stay in contact with me now, though they won't acknowledge Brice, my fiancé. Dad will talk to him, but Mom never even mentions him. They drove up for Noah's birthday party and realized we were living together. Brice's family and our friends were there, and they're all Mexican. They didn't talk to anyone. They just sat in the other room and then left. It was only the second time they'd been up. The first was for a baseball game. That day, when she wanted to say something to Brice, she talked to him through me. Noah and I did get "cordially invited" to Dad's birthday party. They were nice and everything. I just can't bring my fiancé home.

Mom still puts her two cents in, like when I got engaged. Brice is a great guy. He's a hard worker, he actually acts like Noah is his own kid, he wishes he was his, and he pretty much is. Brice can't adopt him because of Rob, but Noah is pretty much Brice's son. Rob, his biological father, isn't even trying. He's been out of the country for a couple of years. He's not even trying to move back. He's engaged, but he doesn't care about Noah. Whenever he has Noah, he just wants to show him off. He comes back once a month, and when he doesn't, I let the grandparents exercise the visitation. He doesn't call every weekend, and when he does, it's when he's on the way to something. He schedules Noah around everything else instead of everything else around Noah. It's nice that I have Brice because he's the father Noah should have had and now does have.

Anyway, Brice proposed on Christmas day. I dreaded calling my mom and dad, which is sad since it was such exciting news, but I knew Mom would say something to piss me off. I called anyway and she said, "Well, are you sure?"

"Yeah Mom," I said, "I'm sure. Like I get proposed to everyday—this happens once. Why can't you just be happy for me?"

"Well I'm glad you're engaged," she said, "but I'm not happy you're still shacking."

I say, "Well Mom, what do you want me to do? Get married today? The courts aren't open. I just got engaged."

"Well, when are you getting married?"

***

I had a miscarriage at the end of November. I'd never had one before. I even posted that I was pregnant online. I'd had two healthy babies, and I thought it was safe to put it out there. I started feeling really weird, and I had a doctor's appointment—we were supposed to be able to hear the heartbeat. We got there and I told him I had had some spotting, which I hadn't had with the other pregnancies.

He told me in advance not to get upset if I didn't hear the heartbeat since it was still a little early. That right there was a warning sign to me. I knew he was only telling me that because I was spotting. We didn't hear a heartbeat, and I think I knew then. That was the hardest, that night, because I had to go in for an ultrasound the next day. They saw the baby, but not a heartbeat. They said I was supposed to be 11-12 weeks, but the baby only looked 7-8 weeks, and they asked over and over if I was sure about my dates. I was sure. The baby looked healthy. The sac wasn't breaking down. Then they did the vaginal ultrasound and there was no heartbeat, so I had to go get a D&C.

I had people in the room with me who thought I was having an abortion. I wanted this baby and I lost it. The nurse even said 'abortion', and I didn't correct him. Then another nurse came in who mentioned it was a miscarriage and you could just see his eyes go, "Oh."

My mom told me when I was pregnant with my first child, that having to give her up for adoption was God's punishment for me having this child out of wedlock. When I told my mom I was pregnant this time, I knew they wouldn't be thrilled, but I wanted them to be happy that I was happy, and my Dad said, "Why would we

141

be happy you're having another child out of wedlock?" He did email to say he was sorry to hear I'd miscarried.

Then, when I had the miscarriage, I told my doctor what my mother believed about having to give my baby up. He told me, "This is not your fault. This is not God punishing you. This has nothing to do with that."

I asked mom if she felt the same way about my miscarriage and she said, "I didn't say that." I had been such an embarrassment to them when I was pregnant the first time. They weren't happy about this pregnancy, so why wouldn't she be relieved that it was over?

***

I'm ready to move out of state. Five or six years ago I thought I'd never be able to do that. I felt so close to my family. Would I miss them? Absolutely, but I've always wanted to move. It would have been really hard before, but now it wouldn't be. I still love my parents, but they've never apologized for kicking me out for dating a Hispanic guy or giving me an ultimatum with my child. So, I don't know how I could forgive them for something like that. I'd like to say I have, but I haven't.

Even so, getting kicked out of my parents' house was probably the best thing that ever happened to me, because I had to learn to do things for myself. Even before I had a child to think of I had to support myself. Slowly but surely I figured out, "Okay, I can do this." I gained more self-confidence because I had to do it. I wasn't crawling back to them. That forced me to swim. I'm too proud and too stubborn to go back for help. Stubbornness and pride can be bad things, but they can also be good. Depends on the situation and I had a lot of stubbornness.

She'll still trying to play mind games, and I just say, "Mom, I'm an adult. I'm not going to just sit here and let you brainwash me. It's not going to work." She's still trying to "fix" my life. I think she feels like a failure as a parent. She feels like she didn't do something right. I've told her before that it has nothing to do with her, but she wants to take it all on herself and feel guilty for whatever reason.

142

Either way, I'm in a good place now. I'm engaged to a good man. You think you could never find someone who's made just for you and then you do. He's never had any problems with Noah. He considers him as his own.

Anna: So with all you've gone through, what would you say to someone in your shoes say 5 or 10 years ago?

Lauren: It depends on the situation. Is your family willing to accept what they don't agree with or are they going to work against you like mine - giving ultimatums for everything? I would say plow through it. If it's like what I went through, don't give up on yourself. You know what's best for you and you know what you feel is right so go for it. I don't think you'll be disappointed in the end result. It may feel like it takes a long time, that the light is never going to be at the end of the tunnel – that this tunnel must be the Wall of China, but it will get better.

If you hit rock bottom, things can only go up. It seemed like it was never going to get better, but I was also really young. I had so much left to do and so much time to do it. No matter what your age, don't ever give up on what you want to do because someone is telling you not to do it. You know your opinions, your heart, your brain, and as long as you're not intentionally hurting others (because I got a lot of that from my family—"Oh you're really putting your mom through a lot," but it wasn't about them or her. They wanted to make it seem like I was making choices to hurt them when I was really making choices for myself. It had nothing to do with them, but they still wanted to guilt trip me), plow through it. Everything will eventually get better. If life were easy it would be boring. It doesn't have to be *that* exciting. I just couldn't cower and do what they wanted me to, even when they brought God into it.

I definitely thought I could have my cake and eat it too. I thought there would be give and take. Every time I went home to them, and when I tried to go back and make things right, I thought that I was giving and eventually they would too, but that's not what happened. It was never about me and my needs, it was about them and what they wanted me to do. They were going to keep taking until it drained me physically, emotionally, mentally. They put the biggest guilt trips on me. That's how it was, but I just kept thinking, "But I love my family. I'm a horrible person if I give up and turn my back on them."

They made it perfectly clear what they think of me and gave up on me long ago. They want me to do what they want me to do and it's not because they love me so much. It's because of how I'm making the family look. I'm disruptive to the family and the family name. They're going to do whatever it takes to get me back because they don't want me out there making the family look bad. After all this time, why would I want to put myself in that position again? I don't regret my decision. I've been through mental and psychological abuse, but never physical. It could have been so much worse. I was naïve enough to think, "They care about me, and they're doing this for me." No. They did it for them.

It may not end up well when you make your own choices, but it could, too. You have to be aware that on this journey things may not turn out the way you want them to, and they may turn out better. I'm the happiest I've been in a long time.

~~~~~~

Lauren's story is a good word of warning for both emerging adults and their parents. It's certainly true that the tighter your parents hold on the harder you push to be free—I can attest to that feeling as well as Lauren and any other person who was once an adolescent/emerging adult. Had Lauren's parents accepted that Lauren wanted something different for her life than they were envisioning, like an interethnic relationship, or had they been more sympathetic when she got into difficult situations, like an unplanned pregnancy, she *may* have landed solidly on her feet sooner rather than later. Even with a baby to care for. Had they sincerely asked her what she wanted for herself, and then supported her choices, things *might* have turned out differently. This would have required Lauren's parents to assess their own fears and do a lot of self-work around the nerve-wracking experience of seeing your child fly off into the world.

Instead, Lauren's parents continued to try to shape her life into what they saw as acceptable for their daughter. Maybe they thought they were preserving her health and happiness by pressuring her into their preferred situation for a young woman. But each person has a different idea of what a happy, healthy, appropriate life looks like. All parents need to remember that they don't get to dictate how their children create their lives, especially when those children have become young adults.

Trying to decide whether Lauren's parents' controlling ways caused her rebelliousness or the other way around is a chicken and the egg scenario. Certainly Lauren's parents would see Lauren's story from a wildly different perspective. Whether their intentions were good or not, their methods proved themselves to be both ineffective and traumatically harmful.

That being said, Lauren's story illustrates many of the pitfalls young women face when they're coming of age. Power struggles with authority figures, unexpected pregnancies, unhealthy relationships, and the often turbulent learning curve toward independence are all issues that many of the young women I know have faced, in varying degrees. Lauren happened to face them in extremes. Regardless of what might have been for Lauren, we're going to allow her story to teach what it takes to create stability as an emerging adult, how to avoid the pitfalls, and how to get yourself out of them when you do fall in.

Even if you have the best, most supportive parents in the world, you will, as you enter into adulthood, have to stand on your own two feet. What supportive parents get you is help out of the pitfalls. Remember Becca's story? She was able to land smoothly on her feet and support her daughter while she was at it because of the support and encouragement she got from her parents. Supportive parents withhold judgment and help you stand on your own. Whether you have supportive parents or not, let's take a look at what we can learn from Lauren's story about emerging gracefully into adulthood and combine that with the abuse resistance and recovery methods covered in the previous sections.

Emerging Adulthood
Trading Pressure for Grace

It seems pretty clear that relationship violence occurs so often between the ages of 18 and 24 because entering adulthood is an unsteady and intense period of development. It's a time when you're enjoying the most freedom and responsibility you've ever had, which is fun, but many people enter these years with virtually no adult life skills. Managing life can get overwhelming quickly. It does not help that many emerging adults feel like the rest of their life is hanging on the choices they make during this period. In a very real sense this is true, but teaching emerging adults that they can ruin their entire lives by making the wrong decisions does not say much for one's faith in redemption or the resiliency of human beings.

People of all ages make big, often passionate, decisions every day that sometimes turn out really well and sometimes turn out poorly. We are all constantly cleaning up the mess from a mistake we made. That's why parents get so stressed out and try to control their young adult's lives. They're scared that their kids will spend a decade cleaning up a mess made in one split second of mindlessness. Clearly, the pressure that is placed on emerging adults to make all the right choices is rooted deeply in fear.

Ironically, it's often the pressure to become successful quickly that pushes emerging adults toward mindlessness. There seems to be this pressure valve that shuts the whole thinking machine down when emerging adults can't see through the thick gravy of pressure being heaped on and around them by parents, teachers, and society in general. The untrained, under-developed instinct kicks on, and whoops! Babies are made. Because that's what humans do. Of course, it's not always a baby, but something happens that complicates life in a big way. These 'complications' are the natural results of numbing out to escape the pressure. They do have the potential to raise you up out of the fear based pressure system—which is a rat race in a hamster wheel—and set you on the path of rational adult survival in a hurry (ask me how I know). However, finding the path before the complication is a much, much, much better idea.

Becoming an adult is easily one of the most difficult yet dynamic and exciting phases you'll ever experience. Even with the most careful, meticulous planning, everyone will make mistakes. Some of the more difficult struggles that can come up as you become an adult are avoidable, like unplanned pregnancies or abusive relationships. The thinking machine has to stay on, though. The thinking machine includes your intelligence, of course, along with your intuition, your good judgement, and your connection to a vision for yourself. It's your sense of knowing.

You can keep your sense of knowing in working order by setting your own standards of excellence, and trading pressure in for grace. Grace combats pressure effectively. Grace knows that you can handle the fallout if you make a mistake. Grace knows that forgiving yourself for making a wrong turn is the fastest way to get back on track. Grace knows that there is no such thing as 'one right way' to get where you want to be. Grace knows that your vision for yourself will clear up as life goes on, and that all the little efforts count. Grace knows that pressure and perfectionism slow you down. Grace is a practice. It is stronger than harsh discipline, and more effective than judgement.

When pressure sees imperfection, grace sees growth, improvement, and learning. When pressure sees failure, grace sees a chance to heal and try again. When pressure demeans, grace lifts up and whispers *begin again*. Grace feels like kindness, forgiveness, and mercy. Grace embraces flexibility. Grace is a muscle we can exercise. When we exercise it over and over and over it becomes stronger than pressure, and we become stronger, too.

So, when pressure begins to pile up messages in your head like, "You've screwed up so badly. You'll never make it. You're not doing enough. You're moving too slow. You aren't good enough," muffle the noise with grace. *I am capable of handling the fallout of that bad decision. Every day I get closer to where I want to be. I did one really good thing today. I am thorough. I am worthy.* And on the days when it feels like not one constructive thing got done, grace says: *Rest your head. Tomorrow is another day.*

Lots of things can get in the way of allowing yourself to live in grace. One of them is the harsh judgement and control of an abuser. Abusers aren't great at grace. They don't give themselves grace, because they don't believe they're worthy of it. That sense of unworthiness gnaws at their personal power, so they grasp for a sense of power through the control and manipulation of others. Of course, this power is counterfeit, so the longing for power is never satiated. Fortunately, deep within the heart of grace lies our worthiness to receive it. All of us. We're all worthy. The catch is that we must begin practicing and receiving grace *before* we believe we're worthy of it. And hear this: If we are worthy of grace, certainly we are worthy of just treatment in our relationships.

Most of us crave relationship. It's biological. With the way that dating works, it's likely you'll need to end some relationships before you settle down with someone you can create a fulfilling relationship with. Inevitably there will be mismatches and periods of loneliness, even if you're having healthy relationships with kind people. We get through this. Love yourself through it, even if you make big mistakes or find that your choices have led to complications. Our desire for love and companionship deserves grace, too.

Steering Your Own Course
Thoughtful Choice-Making vs. Rebellion

Like every other phase of life, emerging adulthood is what you make of it. Some people travel the world. Some people go to college. Some people start a business. The point is that you can make these years whatever you want them to be. They are yours and no one else's. If you have a clear idea of what you want to make of them, be courageous enough to act on your vision.

Some people feel they don't have a choice about how they spend these pivotal years. Maybe their parents have already chosen for them. Maybe it feels like there is only one real, responsible option. It's clear that Lauren's biggest struggle as she became an adult was deciding whether to try to live the life her parents expected of her or to live a life completely on her own.

Lauren stated that she was in a rebellious stage when she got pregnant with Noah. I have to wonder if her experience left room for her to see that there was a middle way between rebellion and subservience. She hadn't had time to grieve her loss, or really plan a future. There was not a lot of space for her to make any decisions at all. When your life is being controlled, the bar for rebellion is set pretty low. Any independent decision could be seen as rebellion. Most of us would not see choosing which school to go to or who to date as rebellious decisions for a 21 year old.

When you've spent your childhood and teen years having someone make all of your decisions for you, being told that your parents know more about what is best for you than you do, you haven't had the chance to figure out what you want or what works for you. This makes for a chaotic entry into adulthood. Especially when your personal beliefs are different from your family's. In some cases, the differences are so profound, like in Lauren's case with her attraction to Hispanic men in a prejudiced family, that it can be next to impossible to reconcile the differences between your family's beliefs and the way you chose to live. Lauren's preferences, and her family's harsh reaction to them, triggered an enormous conflict over who would maintain control of her life.

Whether or not this kind of conflict exists in your life, emerging into adulthood is a time during which we learn to steer our own course. At some point parents have to get out of the driver's seat. Hopefully parents take on a role of guidance and offer wisdom to their children as they start making their way into the world. If the relationship is toxic and controlling, though, you need to be able to take the reins and start maneuvering your way through life on your own, reaching out for guidance from other mentors when you need it.

Learning to steer your own course can start right now, and it's not at all about rebellion. Rebellion tends to happen in spurts of passion, rage, anger or frustration. Steering your own course is more thoughtful. The way you feel when you make a choice for yourself that isn't aligned with what others want for you can be a good reference point to help you decipher whether you're acting out of rebellion or if you're making thoughtful choices. Are you pushing against something or someone, or are you drawing yourself up? Rebellion is likely to create difficult situations in your life. Steering your own course will, if you are consistent, lead you to the life you really want. You may go through some unexpected circumstances along the way, but you will eventually get there.

Ideally, your parents will support and try to understand the decisions you make for yourself. They might point out possible struggles and help you make plans to prepare for those struggles. This would be truly helpful, since your parents have done this whole emerging adulthood thing themselves. In this case, rebellion isn't even an issue. If this is not the case with your parents, though, you should know that you really can make it on your own if you need to. Being independent is not being rebellious. It's being an adult.

We talked a lot about self-care in previous sections, and steering your own course grows out of self-care. It's about taking every decision you face and asking yourself, "What is best for me in this situation? What will lead me to happiness and security?" If you, like Lauren, have a child along the way, the 'me' in those questions becomes 'us'. Be diligent, and careful. Write it out, make a reasonable plan, and then follow through with it. Of course, sometimes things happen and there's no time to plan. Sometimes quick choices are necessary. Be confident in yourself and know that both well thought out plans and quick choices can end in success or turn out badly. It's okay. You get to keep going either way. You get to graciously take responsibility for your choices and adjust to life's twists and turns as necessary.

So, what might practical, responsible choice-making look like when it's not aligned with what your parents want for you? Let's say you start college with the intentions of being a doctor and realize a few semesters in that the idea of being a doctor now makes your skin crawl and you'd rather do something else. You wouldn't have a problem changing majors, but your dad or mom is a doctor and is really excited about you joining their practice when you finally graduate. Steering your own course would mean checking in with yourself, honoring what is best for you, readjusting your sails toward a different career, and then responsibly and lovingly talking to your parent about why you need to change your plans. Then, no matter what is said or done, sticking to your plans to create the life you want to live.

One of the main reasons that people sometimes make decisions to please others rather than do what's right for them is that they don't want to hurt anyone. While this is understandable, all too often it comes back to bite you. The fact is, those choices aren't going to make the other person happy anyway.

Most people who are so invested in the choices of others that they are willing to manipulate or bully people into submission are terribly fearful and insecure themselves. In these cases no amount of submission will satiate their need for security. For whatever reason, controlling and manipulative people seem to find their sense of security in the domination of others. They'll always want the people in their lives to make choices that satisfy them. Like Lauren's mother, who was so fearful that her daughter would live a lifestyle that she could not be proud of or control; nothing but absolute submission on Lauren's part would have satisfied her. Even then, would she really have been happy? Were Lauren's choices really "putting her mother through a lot," as her relatives suggested, or was her mother constantly acting out of fear? If Lauren had been following the family rules, it's likely that her mother would have found something or someone else to worry over or control.

When we allow someone else to steer our course as an adult, meaning we're making decisions that we're not really comfortable with to please or appease someone else, we're allowing fear to dominate our lives. It takes courage to always do what we know is best for us. In the end, it is best for others, too. Even the person we're afraid of hurting. Allowing someone to control us is really just enabling their weaknesses.

The opposite extreme of making choices to please those who manipulate or try to control you is rebellion. I don't think *most* teens or emerging adults rebel just for the fun of it or to blatantly hurt people. It's much more likely that they're rebelling to create a sense of self within a stifling environment. Does rebellion cause pain? Yes, but trying to crush it with more control just exacerbates the cycle. It's interesting to think that an emerging adult could be seen as rebelling against their parents since it infers that their parents are still setting rules or expectations for them to live by.

Regardless, this seems to be the case more and more, and it's important to know that rebelling works about as well as trying to fit the mold another person has made for you. It will backfire in a big way. Rebellion creates chaos. You aren't steering your course because you're only focused on not being what someone else wants you to be. Like fear entrenched pressure, rebellion shuts down your sense of knowing and leaves you reliant on your instinctual brain.

This can surface as lot of anger and impulsivity and will likely land you in a life you had no intention of creating.

As usual, the middle way seems to be the best. Making thoughtful decisions with a lot of good planning to back them up, and a lot of courage and faith to help you stay your own course may be the most difficult path. It's also the most likely way to get where you really want to be. As you make more and more choices for yourself, you grow more confident and learn more about which kind of decisions are effective. Being strong in yourself really just means listening to your own sense of knowing, following through, and handling the fallout of each decision with grace (because there is always fallout even if your decision seems nearly perfect).

Peaceful Emergence

Establishing independence is a painful transition for all parents and emerging adults, but it doesn't have to be like the long drawn out experience Lauren had with her parents. Of course it's going to be painful to say goodbye to someone you've lived with for nearly twenty years, who you've relied on/provided for. It's the perfect opportunity for guilt and regret and old shame to show up for both the parent and the emerging adult. Most of us aren't all that great at processing and letting go of these feelings. Please know that even if your parents are taking their guilt, shame, or regret out on you, that you can still leave home with your peace intact.

No one should have to feel guilty when they're leaving home, or beginning to make their own choices. If you are not released with a blessing, you can still gracefully and mindfully choose independence for yourself. They may see it as rebellion, but you will know that it's not. If you need to, it's okay to love your parents from a distance for a while. Sometimes that's the best situation for everyone.

It's so important to intentionally create the life you want to live, because no one else can live it for you. You don't want to get stuck in a life you hate, and you don't want to someday be the kind of parent who tries to convince your child to live the life you've always dreamed of. Live your own dream life.

Reflection Questions:

1. Can you tell the difference between rebellion and steering your own course? What are your personal clues that let you know if you're acting in your best interest or to "get back" at someone?
2. How do you feel about entering adulthood? Are you excited, scared, ready or wishing you could postpone it?
3. How do you feel about taking responsibility for your own decision making?
4. How do you think your parents are handling/going to handle it?
5. Do you have clear ideas and plans to avoid the pitfalls that are most common during emerging adulthood (power struggles with authority figures, unexpected pregnancies, unhealthy relationships, learning to be independent)?

Trust
The Courageous Life

All of this talk about emerging adulthood may seem to not fit in a book intended for abuse and domestic violence prevention, but I believe the best prevention for abuse and violence is strong, sure, steady adults. That's what it's all about, and that's what self-care and steering your own course create. Knowing the warning signs is just part of the journey. Getting strong enough to walk away when you know it's time is the ongoing part of this work that becomes a lifestyle. It's a lifestyle that will help you endure your experiences, too. Not only can that strength and wisdom lead you out of abusive situations, it can also sustain you while you finish that degree, start that business, write that book, or birth that baby.

Whatever it is you are drawn to, trust it. Trust that you'll be guided. Trust that you are enough, and that you have what it takes to see it through to completion. Life is full of challenges, but there is nothing to fear. You have what it takes to wisely steer yourself through and around the pitfalls that you'll find along the way. There is no need to be afraid of life.

It's especially important to not be afraid to walk away from situations that do not serve you, be it the wrong college program, the wrong romantic partner, the wrong job, whatever. Even if you've invested years in whatever the thing is, you really can just walk away. There will be mourning for time and effort that feels wasted, but when you release what no longer works for you, you make space for what you really want. Every woman who shared their story for this book did exactly that, and I'm so happy that they're all creating the lives they really want now. What bravery. What fierceness.

We all believe you can create the life you want without having to experience the extremes of abuse and violence described in this book. We believe that you deserve awareness, and that no one deserves to experience what we experienced as we emerged into womanhood. We believe the world can change for the better and that it can evolve into a place where abuse is radically reduced, but only if people refuse to mistreat or be mistreated. Only if people speak out and stand up. For that to happen, we all need to know that we are worthy of being treated well. We need to know when something is not right. We need to know that we can trust ourselves, because even if we make a mistake, we are capable of getting back up.

Whatever you want your life to look like, let it be a courageous one. That doesn't mean that you'll never feel afraid. Just don't be afraid to face fear. Fear is going to pop up. It does for everyone. But when it does, don't be afraid to walk toward it and examine it. It will teach you. You'll learn about yourself and then move on stronger and more knowledgeable than you were before. Living a courageous life simply means not being paralyzed by fear, and not allowing fear to bully you into making choices you don't really want to make.

Fierce Solidarity

Committing to living a courageous life takes fierceness...
Showing a heartfelt and powerful intensity.
Turning that heartfelt and powerful intensity inward, toward cultivating ourselves is what gives us the strength to master our fears and steer our own course. The phenomenal Maya Angelou said, "A woman in harmony with her spirit is like a river flowing. She goes where she will without pretense and arrives at her destination prepared to be herself and only herself." That is what all this is about. It is about saying, "I will not be mastered by any person but myself, and I will honor my true nature while I'm at it." When we do this, we're lining ourselves up to live with purpose. When unhealthy relationships, fear-based decision making, or manipulated faith show up in our lives they hinder us, forming a dam in our freely flowing river. We have to be willing to bust the dam up, or even better, defend our river from unwanted debris in the first place. We must throw any random fallen trees away with all the might we can muster, because if our river isn't flowing, not only are we in a troubled and pressure filled state, we also cannot nourish those downriver.

This is an internal practice. It's a choice that no one else can make for us, and it's not something we can fake. It's about making decision after decision to keep our river flowing, to stay in harmony with ourselves, and it is the greatest gift we could possibly give to ourselves and to everyone around us. Because when we practice this, we ever so gradually learn to love better. When our river is flowing it becomes possible for us to stand in strong solidarity with others who will honor our path as we honor theirs. Then we get to stand together and say no to abuse with authority and authenticity because we have worked so hard to say no to violence within ourselves and in our own lives.

Solidarity means when we see a sister in danger we rally with her. Solidarity means we have our sisters standing behind us, with us, and before us. Solidarity is contagious. We all admire strong women, especially when they're invested in each other. We all want to embody that empowered femininity in the way that we live. This takes daily practice.

When the women in this book volunteered to share their stories in an effort to pave a new path for the next wave of emerging women, it empowered me to move forward with this project. Their willingness to stand with me reassured my belief that we do not have to suffer in this way. We can learn from each other in new ways. We can be better teachers, listeners, and supporters. We can communicate more about what womanhood really is, what it asks of us, and we can help members of the next generation to skip the backsliding and destruction that is relationship abuse and violence. We hope you *all* will skip *all* of that and just get on with growing into strong women.

My hope is that this work will be an aid for you as you transition into womanhood. I hope that you will see clearly your own desires and not be afraid to make them a reality. And if those desires don't turn out to be what you thought they'd be, I hope you will love yourself through the disappointment, knowing all the while that you're capable of change and ongoing creation. What you want out of life is worth the effort, and you are worth the effort, too.

Unhealthy relationships may just be the biggest roadblock there is for emerging young woman, and you don't have to take it. You can walk away from anyone and anything. You deserve support, and real, healthy, encouraging love. Anything less is not worthy of your time or attention, because the truth is that the support and love we get from intimate relationships are the icing on the cake. The real nourishment of life comes from your willingness to connect to the truth, the strength, the sacred. . . .

The fierceness within you.

A Quick 'Check Your Relationship' Reference

➢ **Possessiveness** is a sign of low self-esteem, and only your partner can improve his/her self- esteem. Love is not being in the business of fixing people, so don't think it's your job to make someone feel better about themselves. Possessive behavior is never a sign of affection. Love does not mean you belong to each other.

➢ **Jealousy** leads to isolation and control. If s/he's acting jealous, confront them right then and there and make clear that your value for them does not remove your value for others in your life. If the jealous behavior doesn't stop, end things, and don't look back. A relationship based on real love won't need you to give up your friends, family, faith (or non-faith), style, or interests.

➢ **Control** is when a person insists that their partner do what they say. This leads to violence and is a form of truly harmful emotional abuse. If you find your actions or ideas are being manipulated or controlled, end that relationship as soon as you can.

➢ Any type of **name calling** is unacceptable. **Any person who belittles you** clearly isn't with you because they value you. They are with you because they are getting something from you, be it sex, an ego boost, or a sense of control.

➢ **Verbal abuse** is emotional abuse. It is an assault on the whole person, and it is not acceptable. Verbal abuse consists of any words or phrases that attack who you are, your lovability, your capabilities, or your demeanor. It also involves the efforts made to make you feel guilt and/or shame, or responsibility for another person's actions. If something is said that does not lift you up, clearly state that it is unacceptable and won't be tolerated. If it continues, don't tolerate it...walk away no matter who the person is or how much you love them. You're strong enough, and you will find other people who love you without needing to manipulate and belittle you.

➢ **Physical abuse** is never, ever acceptable. Whether it be a jerk, a slap, a punch, a pinch, a grip, a shove, a restraint, a hair pull, anything. Any intentional infliction of physical pain is grounds for the immediate end of a relationship, and no one gets to "take back" an act of violence or say they didn't mean to.

➢ Your body is your own to share only with whom you happily choose, according to your own personal conditions, beliefs, and boundaries. Any type of **coercion or force** is unacceptable and signifies a need to end the relationship immediately.

159

>>Honor Your Boundaries<<

>>Be Your Own Fiercest Advocate<<

>>Steer Your Own Course<<

>>Keep Your Eyes Wide Open<<

>>Live Your Own Dream Life<<

>>You Are Not Alone<<

>>You Have What it Takes<<

>>Speak Well of Yourself<<

>>You Never Have to Say Yes<<

>>Give Yourself Tender Loving Care<<

>>Stand With Your Sisters<<

>>Celebrate<<

>>Embrace Awareness<<

>>Seek Out Your Mentors<<

>>Cultivate Authentic Faith<<

>>Change is Always an Option<<

>>You Are Responsible for You<<

>>Expect People to Treat You Well<<

>>Reject Abuse—Always<<